THE DIABETES

FAST-FIX

SLOW-COOKER

COOKBOOK

Fresh Twists on Family Favorites

NANCY S. HUGHES

American Diabetes Association.

DIRECTOR, BOOK PUBLISHING
Abe Ogden

MANAGING EDITOR
Greg Guthrie

ACQUISITIONS EDITOR
Victor Van Beuren

PRODUCTION MANAGER
Melissa Sprott

COMPOSITION
Sport Creative

COVER DESIGN
Jody Billert

PHOTOGRAPHER
Thigpen Photography

PRINTER
United Graphics, Inc.

Front cover image:
Hearty Chicken Chipotle Stew with Hominy, p. 50

Back cover image:
Strawberry-Kiwi Cake in a Pot, p. 167

The suggestions and information contained in this publication are generally consistent with the *Clinical Practice Recommendations* and other policies of the American Diabetes Association, but they do not represent the policy or position of the Association or any of its boards or committees. Reasonable steps have been taken to ensure the accuracy of the information presented. However, the American Diabetes Association cannot ensure the safety or efficacy of any product or service described in this publication. Individuals are advised to consult a physician or other appropriate health care professional before undertaking any diet or exercise program or taking any medication referred to in this publication. Professionals must use and apply their own professional judgment, experience, and training and should not rely solely on the information contained in this publication before prescribing any diet, exercise, or medication. The American Diabetes Association—its officers, directors, employees, volunteers, and members—assumes no responsibility or liability for personal or other injury, loss, or damage that may result from the suggestions or information in this publication.

Printed in the United States of America
1 3 5 7 9 10 8 6 4 2

♾ The paper in this publication meets the requirements of the ANSI Standard Z39.48-1992 (permanence of paper).

ADA titles may be purchased for business or promotional use or for special sales. To purchase more than 50 copies of this book at a discount, or for custom editions of this book with your logo, contact the American Diabetes Association at the address below, at booksales@diabetes.org, or by calling 703-299-2046.

American Diabetes Association
1701 North Beauregard Street
Alexandria, Virginia 22311

DOI: 10.2337/9781580404556

Library of Congress Cataloging-in-Publication Data

Hughes, Nancy S.
  The diabetes fast-fix slow-cooker cookbook : Fresh twists on family favorites / by Nancy S. Hughes.
     pages cm
  Includes bibliographical references and index.
  ISBN 978-1-58040-455-6 (pbk.)
 1. Diabetes--Diet therapy--Recipes. 2. Electric cooking, Slow--Recipes. 3. Diabetics--Nutrition. I. Title.
  RC662.H836 2013
  641.5'6314--dc23
                                                        2013014119

To my husband, Greg, who is there for me bite after bite after bite. You are always "right on" with your comments no matter what look I give you! You're brave, you're very brave!

To my children and their growing families, Will, Kelly, Molly Catherine, Anna Flynn, Annie, Terry, Jilli, Jesse, Emma, Taft, and Kara. There's always something in the fridge to taste, there's always something in the freezer to take to your homes, and there's always "peanut butter in the pantry" when you just can't taste another test!

This seemingly never-ending buffet of tastings, testings, re-tastings, re-testings, and commentaries is just part of our lives—and there's no end in sight!

Isn't it a fun ride?

TABLE OF CONTENTS

ACKNOWLEDGMENTS

Thanks to Abe Ogden, my editor, my "believer-in-me," my "go-to-guy" when I needed answers
or needed to be listened to. Thanks for helping me bring my ideas to life!

Thanks to Greg Guthrie and Lauren Wilson, my "unmet" editors and silent heroes,
who made my book look like it does right now—in shape and reader-friendly!

Thanks to Melanie McKibbin, for putting order in the office, order on my desk, and sanity
in my head when deadlines and drama occurred. You did all of this with style and smiles!

Thanks to Wes Shepherd for his energy and stamina to work long hours,
for his "team-player" attitude, for finishing my sentences, and for knowing
to just smile when I ask him to do "just one more thing"!

FROM THE AUTHOR

Don't work so hard! Get some help in the kitchen! Plug in that slow cooker, plop in the ingredients, flip the switch, and do something else while it does the work for you! It's great on your stress level whether you're working, playing, or simply trying to keep up with it all!

With this book, I want you to enjoy great-tasting dishes that will bring your stress level down and your healthy food intake up. None of these recipes takes more than a few minutes to prepare and the slow cooker method is effortless.

Just as I say in all of my cookbooks, "if it's easy, you'll do it again and again." I want you to say "I can do *that!*" I'm here for you and that's why I'm writing this book with the American Diabetes Association. We will show you how to prepare easy dishes that will help you stay on track and, more importantly, *want* to stay on track.

Dishes like *Simply Slow Roasted Chicken and Gravy*, *Pub House Dark Roasted Chuck Roast*, *Hometown Hash Brown Casserole*, and *Ooey Gooey Big Brownie Bowl* will leave you wanting to try more recipes. I created these recipes to make you enjoy what you eat and want to make these recipes for your family and your friends… whether they have diabetes or not. They're just good, heart-warming, "home-worthy" dishes.

These meals are quick to fix and take very little work up front. Prepare the meal before work and you may forget that you did anything until you walk through the door at the end of the day and catch a whiff!

I love this book because I purposely created these dishes so that you won't have to feel deprived— you'll feel comfort.

Enjoy my book! It's meant for you and the ones you care about most.

Nancy

INTRODUCTION

Healthy, economical, easy, "comfort on the go" recipes are in high demand. Chefs of all skill levels agree that slow cooking is an easy alternative to spending hours in the kitchen. It saves time, it saves money, and it saves energy!

A slow cooker also provides some much needed comfort at the end of the day. It's like someone's been home all day cooking just for you! The aroma of a hearty meal takes over your senses, instantly pulling your stress level down while your comfort level soars through the roof!

The purpose of this book is to give you 150 recipes that not only bring the tastes and smells of comfort into your home, but also meet the dietary needs of people with diabetes. This is the tool you need to create healthy, delicious dishes that will in turn give you peace of mind knowing that you are staying on track. Your family and friends will benefit from eating healthy, too!

Backed with the knowledge that every single recipe has been approved by the American Diabetes Association, you can cook with absolute confidence!

CHAPTER 1
You'll Want to Know This!

Advantages of a Slow Cooker

You Can Slow Cook That?

Who Are These Recipes For?

Fast Tricks for Slow Cooking
    Technique Tricks
    Fast Flavoring Facts
    Other Smart Stuff

Advantages of a Slow Cooker

We know slow cooker recipes are a big help on a busy day, but did you know that the slow cooker can do more than make a meal for you? Why not make life even easier in the kitchen. Did you know that a slow cooker…

Takes the Heat Out of the Kitchen
- No big pots to steam up the kitchen.
- No need to heat up a whole oven.
- Great for summer meals.
- Cooks other dishes while you're grilling, from appetizers and sides to desserts.

Acts as a Kitchen Assistant
- Gives a helping hand.
- Can be an extra oven or burner.

Gives You the Gift of Time
- Buys you some time. You don't have to watch over it.
- Frees up your stove top and oven.
- Allows you to be out of the kitchen for extended periods of time.

Can Be a Teaching Tool
- Is a good way to cook with kids. It's fun and quick enough to hold their attention. It helps them learn how to measure, pour, and whisk safely.
- Helps beginner cooks build up their confidence.

Saves Flavor, Saves Moisture, Saves Money
- No moisture escapes so the foods actually cook in their own juices rather than being watered down.
- Because it creates a moist heat, foods retain their natural juices. And in turn, the natural juices add a concentrated flavor that would be lost otherwise.
- Tenderizes tough cuts of meat (which are usually more economical) and fibrous vegetables.

Keeps It Hot
- Keeps food hot while other foods are cooking elsewhere.
- Serve buffet foods in a slow cooker to keep them hot longer.
- Make it portable. When entertaining, place the slow cooker in another part of the house, such as the patio or porch. Plug it in to keep it warm and keep the friends and family circulating!
- Use for "to take" dishes. Many recipes transport easily and hold their flavor and heat for quite some time. Cook, go, and serve!

You Can Slow Cook That?

Our slow cookers have been collecting dust and it's time to bring them out from the cupboard! Or buy a new one, for that matter; they are very inexpensive! Start using your slow cooker to make healthier comfort favorites and experiment with new dishes as well! This book will provide you with new techniques and flavor applications so you can take full advantage of this style of cooking.

A common concern many of us have about slow cooker recipes is that they are not necessarily healthy and they sometimes make every-thing taste boiled and even mushy. This book keeps it simple for you with shortcuts and recipes which utilize mainstream ingredients and things you have on hand. These recipes provide healthy, fresh-tasting comfort.

Also, the slow cooker can do more in the kitchen than you would have ever imagined! For example, you can use your slow cooker to:

- Bake a cake!
- Cook corn on the cob!
- Boil water!
- Steam potatoes!

Slow cooker cakes rise properly, and corn comes out sweet and not soggy. Potatoes and corn on the cob are particularly fun to do in the slow cooker. Just wrap them individually in foil to seal in the flavors and pop them in the cooker! No hot oven, no boiling pots of water, great to transport, and slow cookers hold their heat nicely, too!

If you aren't convinced by what a slow cooker can do, take a look at the recipes inside! They will make you want to get cooking!

Who Are These Recipes For?

The recipes in this book are not only for people with diabetes, but also for those who just want to eat healthy, delicious foods.

The ingredients are readily available, the directions are easy to follow, and the recipes require minimal preparation time. This book is great for beginner cooks who want to learn how to cook and eat healthy. It's also great for seasoned cooks who want to try new and healthy slow cooking techniques.

Slow cookers are not just for big families. You don't have to feed an army of people with this cookbook. Many of us are "downsizing" in one way or another, but we still want those "big pot" flavors. Most of these dishes were designed to serve 4, but occasionally there are some that serve more. Leftovers can be reheated easily for sandwiches or sides or frozen for later meals.

These 150 recipes provide a wide range of choices including appetizers, beverages, soups, stews, sandwiches, entrées, sides, and desserts!

Most of the recipes call for a 3 1/2- to 4-quart slow cooker, preferably round. However, some call for a 6-quart, preferably oval, slow cooker. Slow cookers are relatively inexpensive so if you can get both sizes, go for it! The results will be worth it!

Fast Tricks for Slow Cooking

TECHNIQUE TRICKS

USING THE SLOW COOKER AS A MINI-OVEN: Yes, you can treat your slow cooker like a mini-oven! The trick is to place a loaf pan on a rack or several aluminum foil balls to keep it off the bottom of the slow cooker so it will cook evenly!

USING PARCHMENT PAPER: When baking cakes directly in the slow cooker insert, it's best to line the bottom and the sides of the insert with parchment or wax paper. Coat the sides of the insert with cooking spray and mold the parchment paper to the insert. That will prevent the cake from browning too much. It is especially useful if your slow cooker has a hot spot.

USING A 2-CUP MEASURE: You don't need to buy a small slow cooker. You can use a 2-cup heat-resistant glass measuring cup when working with smaller amounts of ingredients, especially for appetizers or toppings. The size fits perfectly into a 3 1/2- to 4-quart slow cooker, it's heat resistant, and it's easy to remove.

REMOVING SKIN FROM CHICKEN: Need to skin a chicken leg or thigh? That can pose a problem, because it's hard to get any traction, but it's important to remove the skin for your health and the quality of your recipe. All you have to do is use paper towels to pull off the skin. This adds a bit of traction to keep your fingers from slipping. Hold the chicken with one paper towel and pull the skin off with another! It's that simple!

MAKING A SLING: Meatloaf can be a bit tricky to remove in one piece from the slow cooker. Take three 18-inch-long sheets of foil and fold each of the sheets in half lengthwise. Coat the foil strips with cooking spray. Crisscross the strips in a spoke-like fashion to act as a sling. Place the loaf in the center of the spokes. Lift the ends of the foil strips to transfer the loaf to the cooker, leaving the foil in place during cooking. Then all you have to do is lift the meatloaf out easily and in one piece!

REMOVING SEEDS: When a recipe calls for removing seeds from squash or even jalapeños, use a small spoon to scrape the seeds and the membranes. If you're working with jalapeños, do this under cold running water to prevent burning yourself.

THAWING VEGETABLES: Need to thaw veggies fast? Place in a colander, run under cold water 20–30 seconds, and shake off excess water.

CUTTING WINTER SQUASH: Acorn and butternut squash are loaded with nutritional benefits, but you might shy away from them because they can be difficult to cut. To make squash easier to cut, pierce the outer skin in several areas with a fork. Place the squash on a paper towel in the microwave and cook on high for about 2 to 2 1/2 minutes, no longer. Place on a cutting board and use a clean dish towel to hold the squash in place while cutting. It cuts right through! Then continue cooking as directed.

Fast Tricks for **Slow** Cooking

FAST FLAVORING FACTS

DOUBLE DUTY: For certain meals, such as chili, reserve some of the fresh ingredients, like onions, peppers, and tomatoes, serve them raw and finely chopped on top of your slow cooked meal with sour cream or a splash of fresh lime. It adds a whole new depth and layer of flavor, providing crunch, color, and freshness!

SNEAK 'EM IN: Some vegetables have a tendency to break down in the slow cooker and simply season the dish so you don't see them! Using these vegetables is a great way to "sneak" important nutrients into your dishes.

ADDING AT THE END:
- Adding spinach into the dish at the end gently and quickly cooks the tender spinach while retaining its brilliant green color. Be sure to add it at the very last second if you want the color to pop!
- Certain ingredients—like olives, fresh herbs, fresh ginger, citrus zest, oil, and salt—are often added at the end of the cooking process to enhance the flavors and textures of the dish. These ingredients can get lost in the dish if added earlier. Not so with dried herbs and spices. They need to be added in the beginning in order to release their flavors.
- Add browned turkey or chicken sausage during the last 15 minutes of cooking time so it retains its complex flavors and texture.

QUICK THICK IT: For more concentrated flavors and to slightly thicken a recipe, simply remove the cover at the end of the cooking time and let it stand for 15 minutes to allow some of the liquid to evaporate. With vegetable-based recipes, you can purée 1–2 cups of the mixture in a blender. It's especially easy with a hand-held immersion blender.

INSTANT COLOR: Foods don't brown in the slow cooker like they do in the oven, so to help achieve a rich color, use herbs and spices, such as paprika, chili powder, or cinnamon.

BRIGHTEN YOUR RICE: Brown rice is delicious, but it can be a bit bland to the eye. Make it pop by adding 1/4 teaspoon ground turmeric to your rice and water. It will turn it a brilliant yellow!

SEASON UP...SOME: Use fresh or dried herbs and spices and salt-free seasoning blends. You can use traditional seasoning packets that are on the market, but be wary of the sodium content. If you choose a brand that does not have a low-sodium option, use half the packet.

COFFEE, THE SECRET INGREDIENT: Fear adding coffee granules to food? Don't! It's perfect if you want to add a deeper beef flavor to a stew, a heartier flavor to chilis, or even a richer chocolate taste to your desserts. It's amazing how it helps step up the flavors!

Fast Tricks for Slow Cooking

FAST FLAVORING FACTS

BROWN, IF YOU CAN: Browning is one step that matters when it comes to bringing out additional natural flavors.

TURN OFF THE HEAT: Some recipes will tell you to turn off the heat and uncover the slow cooker for a few minutes. This allows the flavors to absorb into the dish and allows some of the liquid to evaporate, which changes the flavor and texture of the dish.

TIP OF SUGAR: Sometimes you'll see that a small amount of sugar is added to a recipe. This is not to make the dish sweeter, but to counterbalance the acidity of other ingredients in the dish!

NEXT DAY: A lot of recipes, especially the soups, stews, and roasts, tend to have a more blended flavor the next day. These are great "make ahead" dishes. Keep that in mind when you're having guests over—it will make for easy entertaining!

OTHER SMART STUFF

MEASURE IT UP: Measuring is crucial. The right amount of seasoning or vegetables will give you the right results.

CUT IT RIGHT: Cutting your ingredients as directed is very important. It can make or break your recipe. So pull out the ruler! Yes, the ruler! See what a 1/2 inch is. I think you'll be surprised.

FOLLOW DIRECTIONS WELL: Most recipes may be cooked on either the high or the low setting. Some require the use of only one specific setting, however. Be sure to pay attention to the directions for the best results.

UTILIZE THOSE LAST 15 MINUTES: Add the more delicate ingredients such as shrimp, broccoli, or dairy products during the last 15 minutes of cooking to prevent overcooking or curdling.

BUY WHITE WHOLE-WHEAT FLOUR: Several recipes call for white whole-wheat flour. This type of flour is sold in major supermarkets near the all-purpose flour. It's relatively new on the market and it's great for adding more fiber to a recipe because it is not as coarse as the whole-wheat variety.

STOP CHOPPING SO MUCH: Buy ingredients pre-chopped! It does cost a bit more, but it will help make cooking effortless. If you don't plan on using the whole amount purchased within a day or two, freeze any unused portion for a later use! Check out your produce aisle to see what's available.

Fast Tricks for Slow Cooking

USE SILICONE SPATULAS: Buy one...or two. They don't have to be expensive; any will do as long as it says it is heatproof on the label. They are helpful when trying to stir gently or remove any browned bits from a nonstick skillet.

PARBOIL PREFERRED: My favorite variety of long-grain brown rice is the parboiled variety because it seems to hold its firmness and body better through the slow cooking process.

STOCK UP: When shopping, be sure to buy for more than one slow cooker recipe. Keep things like frozen pepper stir-fry and chicken breasts in your freezer and have a few cans of no-salt-added stewed tomatoes on hand at all times for a quick stew!

CUT IT OUT: Be sure to trim your meats and poultry well, or have your butcher do it for you! If you trim the meat yourself, be sure to look for "pockets" of fat. They are easy to remove but can be found even on lean cuts of meat.

BUY A BIT MORE: When buying meat or poultry, it's often necessary to purchase more than needed. A significant amount of fat may need to be trimmed off of even lean cuts and you could end up with less meat or poultry than you need for the recipe. When purchasing chuck roasts, for example, you should buy approximately 6–8 ounces more than the recipe indicates.

PREP AND CHILL: Not a morning person? Prep a recipe the night before and stick it in the fridge. When you need it, pull it out, plug it in, and go! Keep in mind, you may have to add an extra 30 minutes to your cooking time because the slow cooker insert and all the ingredients were cold to start.

FREEZE STUFF: Leftovers? The majority of the entrées, ragouts, and soups in this book are perfect for storing leftovers in individual serving–size containers and freezing. That way it's even more convenient because you have just the right amount waiting for you anytime you need it.

SWITCH IT UP: A lot of the recipes in the appetizer/snack section can be served as a light lunch. Other snack or beverage recipes may be served as a dessert.

KEEP TIME: Be careful not to overcook poultry or other thin cuts of meat. Timing is important.

LIFT THE LID: Add 15–20 minutes to the cooking time every time you do.

RUNNING LATE: Buy a timer. Plug your slow cooker into the timing apparatus and set it for the time you want the slow cooker to turn off. Just remember that even though the slow cooker is turned off, it is still hot and continues to cook the food. Timers are really best to help you if you're running a few minutes late. If you have a programmable slow cooker, timing is not an issue.

CHAPTER 2
Appetizers, Snacks & Beverages

Rosemary-White Bean Hummus Spread

Black Bean Dip with Goat Cheese

Creamy Artichoke Parmesan Dip

Taco Dip

Marinara Dipping Sauce

Sweet Raspberry-Hot Jalapeño Pepper Jelly

Red Pepper, Red Tomato Bruschetta

Pork Sliders with Espresso au Jus

Spiced Nuts, Seeds, and Sticks

Lemony Dill Snack Mix

Lime-Marinated Mushrooms with Soy

Hoppin' Jalapeño Stuffers

Pineapple BBQ Sausage Rounds

Hot Spiced Blueberry Tea

Hot Pineapple-Apricot Ginger Grog

Hot Java Chocolate

Rosemary-White Bean Hummus Spread

Makes 1 1/4 cups
Serves: 6
Serving Size: 1/4 cup

**Exchanges/
Food Choices:**
1 Starch
1/2 Fat

Calories	110
Calories from Fat	25
Total Fat	2.5g
Saturated Fat	0g
Trans Fat	0g
Monounsaturated Fat	1.5g
Cholesterol	0mg
Sodium	440mg
Potassium	232mg
Total Carbohydrate	16g
Dietary Fiber	4g
Sugars	1g
Protein	6g

15-ounce can no-salt-
added navy beans,
rinsed and drained

1/4 cup diced onion

2 medium garlic cloves,
peeled

1 1/2 teaspoons chopped
fresh rosemary **or**
1/2 teaspoon dried
rosemary

2 tablespoons water

1 tablespoon extra-virgin
olive oil

1/4 teaspoon salt

Nonstick cooking spray

TOPPING
1/2 teaspoon chopped
fresh rosemary **or**
1/8 teaspoon dried
rosemary

1/2 teaspoon grated
lemon zest

1 teaspoon lemon juice

2 teaspoons extra-virgin
olive oil

1   **Place the hummus ingredients in a
blender, secure with lid, and purée
until smooth.**

2   **Coat a 2-cup glass measuring
cup or ovenproof bowl with
cooking spray.** Place the hummus
ingredients in the measuring cup.
Place the cup in a 3 1/2- to 4-quart
slow cooker.

3   **Cover the slow cooker and cook
on high for 2 hours, or on low for
3 1/2–4 hours, or until onions are
tender.**

4   **Remove the cup from the slow
cooker.** Place the hummus in a
shallow serving bowl and cool
completely.

5   **At time of serving, combine the
topping ingredients in a small
bowl and spoon on top of the bean
mixture.**

Cook's Note:
Slow cooking the hummus allows
the onion and garlic to cook gently
and provide mellow flavors to the
dish.

Black Bean Dip with Goat Cheese

Makes 2 cups dip
Serves: 8
Serving Size: 1/4 cup

**Exchanges/
Food Choices:**
1/2 Starch

Calories	35
Calories from Fat	0
Total Fat	0g
Saturated Fat	0g
Trans Fat	0g
Monounsaturated Fat	0g
Cholesterol	0mg
Sodium	180mg
Potassium	164mg
Total Carbohydrate	8g
Dietary Fiber	3g
Sugars	1g
Protein	2g

BEAN DIP
Nonstick cooking spray

15-ounce can reduced-sodium black beans, rinsed and drained

1/4 cup diced red onion

1/4 cup chopped cilantro

1 medium garlic clove, peeled

1/4 cup water

2 tablespoons lime juice

1/2 teaspoon ground cumin

1/4 teaspoon salt

1/8 teaspoon cayenne pepper

TOPPING
1 1/2 ounces goat cheese, crumbled

1/2 cup grape tomatoes, quartered

2 tablespoons chopped cilantro

1 **Place the bean dip ingredients in a blender, secure with lid, and purée until smooth.**

2 **Coat a 2-cup glass measuring cup or ovenproof bowl with cooking spray.** Spoon the puréed mixture into the measuring cup. Place the measuring cup in a 3 1/2- to 4-quart slow cooker.

3 **Cover the slow cooker and cook on high for 2 hours, or on low for 3 1/2–4 hours, or until onions are tender.** Remove the cup from the slow cooker.

4 **Place the bean dip in a shallow serving bowl and top with the cheese, tomatoes, and cilantro.** Let stand 5 minutes to absorb flavors and allow the cheese to melt slightly.

5 **Serve warm or room temperature.**

Cook's Note:
The addition of goat cheese gives the dish a taste of "authenticity"!

Creamy Artichoke Parmesan Dip

Makes 3 cups
Serves: 12
Serving Size: 1/4 cup

**Exchanges/
Food Choices:**
1 Vegetable
1/2 Fat

Calories	70
Calories from Fat	40
Total Fat	4.5g
Saturated Fat	1g
Trans Fat	0g
Monounsaturated Fat	0.5g
Cholesterol	5mg
Sodium	280mg
Potassium	16mg
Total Carbohydrate	4g
Dietary Fiber	0g
Sugars	1g
Protein	3g

Nonstick cooking spray

14-ounce can quartered artichoke hearts, drained and coarsely chopped

10-ounce package frozen chopped spinach, thawed but not drained

1/2 cup diced onion

2 medium garlic cloves, minced

1 teaspoon dried oregano leaves

1/2 cup light mayonnaise

1/2 cup grated Parmesan cheese

1 Coat a 3 1/2- to 4-quart slow cooker with cooking spray.

2 Combine the artichokes, spinach and its liquid, onions, garlic, and oregano in the slow cooker.

3 Cover and cook on high for 1 1/2 hours or on low for 2 1/2–3 hours.

4 Stir in the remaining ingredients.

Cook's Note:
Serve with baked pita wedges or on Belgian endive leaves, if desired.

Taco Dip

Makes about 4 cups
Serves: 16
Serving Size: 1/4 cup

**Exchanges/
Food Choices:**
1/2 Carbohydrate
1 Lean Meat

Calories	70
Calories from Fat	20
Total Fat	2g
Saturated Fat	1g
Trans Fat	0g
Monounsaturated Fat	0g
Cholesterol	15mg
Sodium	190mg
Potassium	72mg
Total Carbohydrate	7g
Dietary Fiber	1g
Sugars	1g
Protein	6g

Nonstick cooking spray

8 ounces extra-lean ground beef

1 medium poblano chili pepper, seeded and diced

1 cup frozen corn

1/2 cup diced onion

14.5-ounce can no-salt-added diced tomatoes, drained

1/2 15-ounce can reduced-sodium black beans, rinsed and drained

1-ounce package 40%-less-sodium taco seasoning

1 teaspoon ground cumin

1/4 cup chopped fresh cilantro leaves

1 cup shredded reduced-fat sharp Cheddar cheese

1 **Coat a 3 1/2- to 4-quart slow cooker with cooking spray.**

2 **Heat a medium nonstick skillet coated with cooking spray over medium-high heat.** Brown the beef about 3 minutes, stirring frequently.

3 **Place the beef in the slow cooker with the chili pepper, corn, onions, tomatoes, beans, taco seasoning, and cumin.** Stir until well blended. Cover and cook on low only for 3 hours.

4 **Turn off heat.** Stir in the cilantro and cheese. Cover and let stand 5 minutes to absorb flavors.

Cook's Note:

It's important to cook this recipe on low heat only because the higher heat will curdle the cheese, giving it an undesirable texture. May serve with raw vegetables or baked tortilla chips.

Marinara Dipping Sauce

Makes 3 1/2 cups
Serves: 14
Serving Size: 1/4 cup

**Exchanges/
Food Choices:**
1/2 Carbohydrate
1 Fat

Calories	80
Calories from Fat	35
Total Fat	4g
Saturated Fat	0.5g
Trans Fat	0g
Monounsaturated Fat	1g
Cholesterol	10mg
Sodium	340mg
Potassium	44mg
Total Carbohydrate	8g
Dietary Fiber	1g
Sugars	5g
Protein	4g

Nonstick cooking spray

7 ounces hot Italian turkey sausage or chicken sausage

1/2 cup water

2 cups prepared spaghetti sauce

8-ounce can no-salt-added tomato sauce

1/2 cup diced onion

1/2 teaspoon garlic powder

1 tablespoon dried basil leaves

2 teaspoons dried oregano leaves

1 tablespoon balsamic vinegar

2 teaspoons sugar

2 tablespoons extra-virgin olive oil

1/4 cup grated Parmesan cheese

1   **Coat a 3 1/2- to 4-quart slow cooker with cooking spray.**

2   **Heat a large nonstick skillet coated with cooking spray over medium-high heat.** Brown the sausage, breaking up large pieces while cooking. Place in the slow cooker. To the pan residue in the skillet, add the water and scrape bottom and sides to remove any brown bits. Add to the slow cooker with the remaining ingredients, except the oil and cheese. Cover and cook on high 2 1/2 hours or on low 4 1/2–5 hours or until onions are tender. Stir in the oil and sprinkle with the cheese.

Cook's Note:

Serve with raw vegetables, such as small whole mushrooms, bell pepper strips, zucchini slices, or thin bread sticks, if desired. This freezes well. It may also be used as a sauce for whole-grain pasta using 1/2 cup sauce to 1 cup cooked pasta per serving.

Sweet Raspberry-Hot Jalapeño Pepper Jelly

Makes 1 1/2 cups
Serves: 24
Serving Size: 1 tablespoon

**Exchanges/
Food Choices:**
1/2 Carbohydrate

Calories	35
Calories from Fat	0
Total Fat	0g
Saturated Fat	0g
Trans Fat	0g
Monounsaturated Fat	0g
Cholesterol	0mg
Sodium	0mg
Potassium	5mg
Total Carbohydrate	8g
Dietary Fiber	0g
Sugars	7g
Protein	0g

Nonstick cooking spray

1 cup raspberry fruit spread

1/2 cup frozen unsweetened raspberries

1 medium jalapeño pepper, stem removed and finely chopped, with seeds

2 tablespoons diced red onion

1 tablespoon cider vinegar

1 tablespoon water

2 tablespoons cornstarch

1 tablespoon pourable sugar substitute, such as Splenda, *optional*

1   **Coat a 2-cup glass measuring cup or ovenproof bowl with cooking spray.** Place the fruit spread, raspberries, jalapeño, and onions in the measuring cup.

2   **Place the measuring cup in a 3 1/2- to 4-quart slow cooker.** Cover the slow cooker and cook on high for 2 hours, or on low for 3 1/2–4 hours, or until onions are tender.

3   **In a small bowl, stir together the vinegar, water, and cornstarch.** Stir into the fruit spread mixture, cover, and cook on high 15 minutes to thicken.

4   **Carefully remove the cup from the slow cooker.** Pour the mixture in a shallow serving bowl and allow to cool completely. For a sweeter jelly, stir in the sugar substitute when cooled.

Cook's Note:

May serve 1/2 cup of pepper jelly over 8 ounces fat-free cream cheese with crisp pear or apple slices or whole-grain crackers. Cover and refrigerate leftover pepper jelly for up to 1 month.

Red Pepper, Red Tomato Bruschetta

Makes 1 1/2 cups
Serves: 6
Serving Size: 1/4 cup

**Exchanges/
Food Choices:**
1 Starch
1/2 Fat

Calories	110
Calories from Fat	25
Total Fat	2.5g
Saturated Fat	0g
Trans Fat	0g
Monounsaturated Fat	1.5g
Cholesterol	0mg
Sodium	440mg
Potassium	232mg
Total Carbohydrate	16g
Dietary Fiber	4g
Sugars	1g
Protein	6g

Nonstick cooking spray

1 cup diced red bell pepper

1 cup grape tomatoes, quartered

1/8 teaspoon crushed red pepper flakes

1/2 14-ounce can artichoke hearts, drained and chopped

1 tablespoon chopped fresh oregano or fresh basil

1 medium garlic clove, minced

1 tablespoon extra-virgin olive oil

2 teaspoons red wine vinegar

1/8 teaspoon salt

1/3 cup crumbled reduced-fat feta cheese

1 **Coat a 2-cup glass measuring cup or ovenproof bowl with cooking spray.**

2 **Place the bell pepper, tomatoes, and pepper flakes in the measuring cup.** Place the measuring cup in a 3 1/2- to 4-quart slow cooker.

3 **Cover the slow cooker and cook on high for 1 1/2 hours, or on low for 2 1/2–3 hours, or until peppers are tender.** Carefully remove the cup from the slow cooker, place the mixture in a shallow serving bowl, and allow to cool, about 30 minutes.

4 **Gently stir in the remaining ingredients, except the cheese.** Sprinkle with the cheese.

Cook's Note:
Serve with thin slices of whole-grain baguette bread, or whole-grain cracker, if desired.

Pork Sliders with Espresso au Jus

Makes 12 ounces cooked pork, 1/2 cup juices, and 16 rolls
Serves: 8
Serving Size: 1 1/2 ounces cooked pork, 1 tablespoon juices, and 2 rolls

Exchanges/ Food Choices:
1 1/2 Starch
2 Lean Meat

Calories	180
Calories from Fat	35
Total Fat	4g
Saturated Fat	0g
Trans Fat	0g
Monounsaturated Fat	.05g
Cholesterol	35mg
Sodium	370mg
Potassium	255mg
Total Carbohydrate	23g
Dietary Fiber	0g
Sugars	0g
Protein	21g

Nonstick cooking spray

2 teaspoons instant coffee granules, preferably espresso variety

1 teaspoon onion powder

1/2 teaspoon black pepper

1/4 teaspoon salt, divided

1 pound pork tenderloin

1 teaspoon canola oil

1/4 cup water

1 tablespoon Worcestershire sauce

16 1-ounce whole-grain rolls, split

1 **Coat a 3 1/2- to 4-quart slow cooker with cooking spray.**

2 **In a small bowl, combine the coffee granules, onion powder, black pepper, and 1/8 teaspoon salt.** Coat all sides of the pork with the coffee granule mixture. Press with fingertips to adhere.

3 **Heat the oil in a large nonstick skillet over medium-high heat.** Tilt the skillet to coat the bottom lightly. Brown the pork 3 minutes, turning occasionally.

4 **Remove the skillet from the heat.** Place the pork in the slow cooker. Pour the water and Worcestershire sauce in the skillet, scraping the bottom and sides to remove any browned bits, and pour around the pork.

5 **Cook, covered, on high for 1 hour and 10 minutes, or on low for 2 hours and 15 minutes to 2 1/2 hours, or until the pork registers 145°F on a meat thermometer.** Do not cook longer; the temperature will continue to rise while standing.

6 **Place pork on a cutting board and let stand 10 minutes before thinly slicing.** Stir in remaining salt to drippings and pour evenly over the pork or serve alongside, if preferred. Serve on rolls.

Spiced Nuts, Seeds, and Sticks

Makes 4 cups
Serves: 12
Serving Size: 1/3 cup

**Exchanges/
Food Choices:**
1/2 Carbohydrate
2 Fat

Calories	130
Calories from Fat	80
Total Fat	9g
Saturated Fat	1g
Trans Fat	0g
Monounsaturated Fat	4.5g
Cholesterol	0mg
Sodium	80mg
Potassium	93mg
Total Carbohydrate	10g
Dietary Fiber	2g
Sugars	4g
Protein	3g

Nonstick cooking spray

2 ounces (1/2 cup) chopped pecan pieces

2 ounces (1/2 cup) slivered almonds

2 ounces salted pumpkin seeds, in shells

2 ounces fat-free mini-pretzels

2 teaspoons grated orange zest

1/2 cup dried cranberries

2 teaspoons canola oil

1/8 teaspoon cayenne

2 tablespoons packed brown sugar substitute blend, such as Splenda

1 **Coat a 3 1/2- to 4-quart slow cooker with cooking spray.**

2 **Combine the pecans, almonds, pumpkin seeds, and pretzels in the slow cooker.** Cover and cook on high for 1 hour and 45 minutes, or on low for 3–3 1/2 hours, stirring midway.

3 **Stir in remaining ingredients until well blended.** Place on a large baking sheet in a thin layer to cool completely.

Cook's Note:
Store in an airtight container for up to 2 weeks for peak flavor and texture. Or store in snack-size baggies in 1/3-cup increments for portion control.

Lemony Dill Snack Mix

Makes 8 cups
Serves: 16
Serving Size: 1/2 cup

**Exchanges/
Food Choices:**
1 Starch
1/2 Fat

Calories	140
Calories from Fat	60
Total Fat	7g
Saturated Fat	1g
Trans Fat	0g
Monounsaturated Fat	2.5g
Cholesterol	0mg
Sodium	290mg
Potassium	122mg
Total Carbohydrate	19g
Dietary Fiber	3g
Sugars	2g
Protein	4g

Nonstick cooking spray

1 cup pita chips, broken into bite-size pieces

4 cups Wheat Chex–style cereal

1 cup bagel chips, broken into bite-size pieces

2 ounces (1/2 cup) unsalted peanuts

1/2 cup chopped walnuts

2 tablespoons extra-virgin olive oil

2 tablespoons Dijon mustard

1 tablespoon lemon juice

2 tablespoons grated lemon zest

2 tablespoons dried dill weed

2 teaspoons dried oregano leaves

2 teaspoons onion powder

1 teaspoon garlic powder

3/4 teaspoon salt

1 **Coat a 6-quart slow cooker with cooking spray.** Combine the pita chips, cereal, bagel chips, and nuts in the slow cooker.

2 **In a small bowl, whisk together the oil, mustard, and lemon juice.** Spoon over the cereal mixture and toss gently until well blended. Sprinkle the remaining ingredients, except the salt, over all. Toss until well blended.

3 **Cover and cook on high for 1 hour, stirring every 20 minutes, or on low for 2 hours, stirring every 40 minutes.**

4 **Remove from the slow cooker and place in a thin layer on a large baking sheet or sheet of foil.** Sprinkle the salt evenly over all and let cool 2 hours. Store in airtight container for up to 1 month.

Cook's Note:
The mustard mixture may be a bit thick, but it will distribute during the cooking process.

Lime-Marinated Mushrooms with Soy

Makes 2 cups
Serves: 4
Serving Size: 1/2 cup

**Exchanges/
Food Choices:**
1 Vegetable
1/2 Fat

Calories	60
Calories from Fat	25
Total Fat	3g
Saturated Fat	0g
Trans Fat	0g
Monounsaturated Fat	1.5g
Cholesterol	0mg
Sodium	320mg
Potassium	382mg
Total Carbohydrate	6g
Dietary Fiber	1g
Sugars	4g
Protein	5g

Nonstick cooking spray

1 pound whole mushrooms, wiped clean with damp cloth

2 1/2 tablespoons light soy sauce

2 tablespoons lime juice

2 teaspoons extra-virgin olive oil

3 medium garlic cloves, minced

1/4 teaspoon dried pepper flakes

2 tablespoons finely chopped fresh parsley

1 **Coat a 6-quart slow cooker with cooking spray.** Place the mushrooms in the slow cooker.

2 **In a small bowl, whisk together the soy sauce, lime juice, oil, garlic, and pepper flakes.** Spoon half of the soy sauce mixture over the mushrooms and toss to coat. Cover and cook on high for 3 hours or on low for 6 hours.

3 **Remove the mushrooms with a slotted spoon, discarding the pan drippings.** Spoon the reserved soy sauce mixture over all. Sprinkle with the parsley and toss to coat. Serve hot, room temperature, or chilled. Serve with wooden picks.

Hoppin' Jalapeño Stuffers

Makes 18 pepper halves
Serves: 6
Serving Size: 3 pepper halves

**Exchanges/
Food Choices:**
1/2 Carbohydrate
1 Lean Meat

Calories	80
Calories from Fat	30
Total Fat	3g
Saturated Fat	1.5g
Trans Fat	0g
Monounsaturated Fat	0g
Cholesterol	15mg
Sodium	400mg
Potassium	44mg
Total Carbohydrate	6g
Dietary Fiber	0g
Sugars	1g
Protein	5g

Nonstick cooking spray

1/2 cup frozen brown rice, thawed

1 1/2 ounces light cream cheese

1 1/2 ounces turkey pepperoni slices, finely chopped

1 tablespoon finely chopped fresh parsley

1 teaspoon dried oregano leaves

1/4 cup water

9 medium to large jalapeño chili peppers, trimmed, halved lengthwise, and seeded

1/8 teaspoon salt

1/4 cup finely shredded reduced-fat sharp Cheddar cheese

1   **Coat a 6-quart slow cooker with cooking spray.** Stir together the rice, cream cheese, pepperoni, parsley, and oregano in a medium bowl. Spoon equal amounts in each of the pepper halves.

2   **Put water in the slow cooker and arrange the pepper halves in the bottom, filling side up.** Cover and cook on low only for 3 hours or until peppers are tender.

3   **Turn off the heat, remove cover, and let stand 10 minutes to absorb any liquid.** Carefully remove the peppers from the slow cooker and place on a serving platter. Sprinkle evenly with the salt and the Cheddar cheese. Serve warm or at room temperature.

Cook's Note:

Be sure to wear plastic gloves or cover your fingers with baggies before removing the seeds and membrane of the jalapeños. The juices from the peppers will burn. Another tip is to flush out the seeds and membranes quickly by working with the peppers under running water. Use a 1/4-teaspoon measuring spoon to scrape the seeds and membranes easily.

Pineapple BBQ Sausage Rounds

Makes 2 cups
Serves: 6
Serving Size: 1/3 cup

**Exchanges/
Food Choices**:
1 Carbohydrate
1 Lean Meat

Calories	120
Calories from Fat	30
Total Fat	3.5g
Saturated Fat	0.5g
Trans Fat	0g
Monounsaturated Fat	1g
Cholesterol	20mg
Sodium	220mg
Potassium	119mg
Total Carbohydrate	18g
Dietary Fiber	2g
Sugars	11g
Protein	6g

Nonstick cooking spray

3 tablespoons blackberry fruit spread

2 tablespoons hickory-smoked barbeque sauce

1 teaspoon sugar

2 teaspoons cider vinegar

1/2 teaspoon ground allspice

1/8 teaspoon dried pepper flakes

1 teaspoon canola oil

6 ounces smoked turkey sausage, cut into 32 thin slices

8-ounce can pineapple tidbits, in own juice, drained and patted dry

8-ounce can sliced water chestnuts, drained and patted dry

1 **Coat a 3 1/2- to 4-quart slow cooker with cooking spray.** Stir together the fruit spread, barbeque sauce, sugar, vinegar, allspice, and pepper flakes in slow cooker.

2 **Heat the oil in a large nonstick skillet over medium-high heat.** Brown the sausage, about 4 minutes. Place the sausage in the slow cooker; toss to coat. Cover and cook on high for 1 1/2 hours, or on low for 3 hours, or until richly glazed.

3 **Stir in the pineapple and water chestnuts, cover, and cook on high for 5 minutes to heat through.** Serve hot or room temperature, with wooden picks.

Hot Spiced Blueberry Tea

Makes 9 cups
Serves: 12
Serving Size: 3/4 cup

**Exchanges/
Food Choices:**
1 1/2 Carbohydrate

Calories	100
Calories from Fat	0
Total Fat	0g
Saturated Fat	0g
Trans Fat	0g
Monounsaturated Fat	0g
Cholesterol	0mg
Sodium	15mg
Potassium	45mg
Total Carbohydrate	20g
Dietary Fiber	1g
Sugars	16g
Protein	0g

3 cups blueberry-pomegranate juice

1 1/2 cups red wine **or** 1 cup blueberry-pomegranate juice and 1/2 cup water

5 cups water

1 medium orange, cut into thin rounds

1/2 cup sugar

3 cinnamon sticks

8 whole cloves

1 tablespoon vanilla extract

3 regular-size tea bags

1 **Combine the pomegranate juice, wine, water, orange slices, sugar, cinnamon sticks, and cloves in a 3 1/2- to 4-quart slow cooker.** Cover and cook on high for 3 hours or on low for 6 hours.

2 **Place a colander over a large bowl.** Drain the pomegranate mixture and discard orange slices and spices.

3 **Return the liquid to the slow cooker, stir in the vanilla, and drop the tea bags into the liquid.** Cover and let stand 3 minutes. Remove the tea bags. Serve hot or cold.

Cook's Note:
Do not allow the tea bags to steep longer than 3 minutes or the liquid will become bitter. You can freeze the leftovers without the spices or oranges in an airtight container.

Hot Pineapple-Apricot Ginger Grog

Makes 7 cups
Serves: 9
Serving Size: 3/4 cup

**Exchanges/
Food Choices:**
2 Fruit

Calories	110
Calories from Fat	0
Total Fat	0g
Saturated Fat	0g
Trans Fat	0g
Monounsaturated Fat	0g
Cholesterol	0mg
Sodium	0mg
Potassium	247mg
Total Carbohydrate	28g
Dietary Fiber	1g
Sugars	23g
Protein	1g

46-ounce can unsweetened pineapple juice

1 1/2 cups apricot nectar

2 tablespoons sugar

1 3-inch piece peeled fresh gingerroot

8 whole cloves

1 medium lemon, thinly sliced into rounds and halved

1 **Combine the pineapple juice, apricot nectar, sugar, ginger, and cloves in a 3 1/2- to 4-quart slow cooker.** Cover and cook on high for 3 hours or on low for 6 hours.

2 **Stir in the lemon slices, cover, and cook on high for 15 minutes.**

3 **Serve warm or chilled.**

Cook's Note:

For a more intense ginger flavor, use two 3-inch pieces of ginger.

Hot Java Chocolate

Makes 6 cups
Serves: 8
Serving Size: 3/4 cup

**Exchanges/
Food Choices:**
1 1/2 Carbohydrate
1/2 Fat

Calories	120
Calories from Fat	25
Total Fat	3g
Saturated Fat	1.5g
Trans Fat	0g
Monounsaturated Fat	0g
Cholesterol	5mg
Sodium	210mg
Potassium	233mg
Total Carbohydrate	21g
Dietary Fiber	1g
Sugars	11g
Protein	3g

Nonstick cooking spray

3 cups fat-free half-and-half

2 cups water

1/4 cup packed brown sugar substitute blend, such as Splenda

1/4 cup unsweetened cocoa powder

1/4 cup instant coffee granules, preferably espresso variety

1/4 teaspoon salt

2 cups fat-free whipped topping

1 ounce bittersweet chocolate, broken into small pieces **or** 2 1/2 tablespoons bittersweet chocolate chips

3/4 teaspoon vanilla extract

Peppermint extract, *optional*

1 **Coat a 3 1/2- to 4-quart slow cooker with cooking spray.**

2 **Whisk together the half-and-half, water, brown sugar substitute, cocoa powder, instant coffee granules, and salt in the slow cooker.** Cover and cook on low only for 2 hours.

3 **Whisk in the whipped topping, cover, and cook on low for 10 minutes.** Whisk in the chocolate and vanilla until melted and well blended. If desired, add a few drops of the peppermint extract to each cup.

CHAPTER 3
Sandwiches, Wraps, and More

Chipotle Raspberry Pulled Chicken

Asian Bundle Lettuce Wraps

Chicken and Roasted Garlic Aioli Pitas

Smothered Triple-Onion Brisket Sandwiches

Veggie-Packed, Very Sloppy Joes

Taco Night Filling

Pork-Cilantro Tortillas

Sweet Smoky Pork Tortillas

Tangy Sweet BBQ Pork

No-Fried "Refried" Black Beans

White Bean Crostini

Lima Bean Hummus Pile Ups

Eggplant-Garbanzo Lettuce Wraps

Chipotle Raspberry Pulled Chicken

Makes 4 cups
Serves: 8
Serving Size: 1/2 cup

**Exchanges/
Food Choices:**
1 1/2 Carbohydrate
4 Lean Meat

Calories	290
Calories from Fat	70
Total Fat	8g
Saturated Fat	2g
Trans Fat	0g
Monounsaturated Fat	3g
Cholesterol	90mg
Sodium	530mg
Potassium	457mg
Total Carbohydrate	23g
Dietary Fiber	1g
Sugars	18g
Protein	27g

Nonstick cooking spray

2 cups diced onion

1/4 cup balsamic vinegar

2 medium chipotle peppers (canned in adobo sauce), mashed with a fork and minced

1 tablespoon adobo sauce (sauce from chipotle peppers)

1 teaspoon garlic powder

1/2 teaspoon black pepper

1 pound boneless, skinless, chicken breasts, trimmed of fat

1 pound boneless, skinless, chicken thighs, trimmed of fat

1/2 cup raspberry fruit spread

1/2 cup low-sodium hickory or mesquite barbeque sauce

1 **Coat a 3 1/2- to 4-quart slow cooker with cooking spray.** Place onions on bottom of the slow cooker.

2 **In a small bowl, stir together the vinegar, chipotle peppers, adobo sauce, garlic, and black pepper.**

3 **Place half of the chicken in the slow cooker on top of the onions.** Spoon half of the vinegar mixture over the chicken. Repeat with the remaining chicken pieces and vinegar mixture. Cover and cook on high for 2 1/2 hours or on low for 5 hours.

4 **Remove the chicken with a slotted spoon and shred.** Place a colander in a medium bowl. Pour the onion mixture into the colander and drain well.

5 **Return the onion mixture in the colander to the slow cooker with the chicken.** Discard the liquid in the bowl. Stir the fruit spread and barbeque sauce into the onion mixture. Cover and cook on high 15 minutes to absorb flavors.

Asian Bundle Lettuce Wraps

Makes 3 cups pork mixture
Serves: 4
Serving Size: 3 lettuce leaves, 3/4 cup coleslaw, and 3/4 cup pork mixture

Exchanges/ Food Choices:
1 Carbohydrate
2 Vegetable
4 Lean Meat
1/2 Fat

Calories	320
Calories from Fat	80
Total Fat	9g
Saturated Fat	2.5g
Trans Fat	0g
Monounsaturated Fat	3g
Cholesterol	100mg
Sodium	590mg
Potassium	653mg
Total Carbohydrate	24g
Dietary Fiber	3g
Sugars	15g
Protein	35g

Nonstick cooking spray

1 cup diced onion

1 1/2 pounds boneless pork chops, trimmed of fat

1/4 cup light soy sauce

1/4 teaspoon dried pepper flakes

1 1/2 tablespoons cornstarch

2 tablespoons water

2 1/2 tablespoons granulated sugar

2 teaspoons curry powder

1/4 cup lime juice

3 cups packaged cabbage-and-carrot coleslaw

12 large Boston lettuce leaves

1/2 cup thinly sliced red onion

1/2 cup chopped fresh cilantro leaves

1 **Coat a 3 1/2- to 4-quart slow cooker with cooking spray.** Place the onions in the bottom of the slow cooker, top with the pork, soy sauce, and pepper flakes. Cover and cook on high for 3 hours, or on low for 6 hours, or until pork is tender.

2 **Remove the pork with a large slotted spoon and place on cutting board.**

3 **In a small bowl, combine the cornstarch and water.** Stir until cornstarch is completely dissolved. Stir into the slow cooker with the sugar, curry, and lime juice. Shred meat and return to the slow cooker. Cover and cook on high 15 minutes or until thickened.

4 **Place coleslaw in lettuce leaves and top with the pork mixture, red onions, and cilantro.**

Chicken and Roasted Garlic Aioli Pitas

Makes 4 pitas
Serves: 4
Serving Size: 1 pita half,
3 ounces cooked chicken,
1/2 cup lettuce, and
2 tablespoons feta

**Exchanges/
Food Choices:**
1 Starch
1/2 Carbohydrate
2 Lean Meat
1 Fat

Calories	260
Calories from Fat	80
Total Fat	9g
Saturated Fat	2.5g
Trans Fat	0g
Monounsaturated Fat	1.5g
Cholesterol	45mg
Sodium	540mg
Potassium	421mg
Total Carbohydrate	26g
Dietary Fiber	5g
Sugars	3g
Protein	19g

Nonstick cooking spray

2 medium lemons, divided

4 4-ounce boneless,
skinless chicken
breasts, trimmed of fat

1/2 teaspoon dried
oregano leaves

1/4 teaspoon dried
rosemary

4 medium garlic cloves,
peeled

1/4 cup light mayonnaise

2 tablespoons fat-free
milk

2 cups chopped romaine
lettuce

2 whole-wheat pita
rounds, cut in half
crosswise

1/2 cup thinly sliced red
onion

1/4 teaspoon black pepper

1/2 cup crumbled,
reduced-fat feta cheese

1 **Coat a 3 1/2- to 4-quart slow
cooker with cooking spray.**
Slice one of the lemons into thin
rounds. Place the lemon slices on
the bottom of the slow cooker,
overlapping slightly, if necessary.

2 **Place the chicken on top of the
lemons and sprinkle with the
oregano and rosemary.** Place
garlic cloves around the chicken.
Cover and cook on high for 1 hour
and 15 minutes, or on low for
2 1/2 hours, or until chicken is no
longer pink in center.

3 **Remove the chicken and place on
cutting board.** Remove the garlic
and place in a medium bowl with
the mayonnaise, milk, and
3 tablespoons of the pan drippings.
Stir until smooth. The garlic will
break down while stirring. Shred the
chicken, discarding lemon slices
and remaining pan drippings in pot.

4 **To serve, place the lettuce in the
pita halves, top with the red onion,
mayonnaise mixture, chicken, black
pepper, and feta.** Cut the remaining
lemon into wedges and serve with
the pitas to squeeze over all.

Cook's Note:
For a variation, use reduced-fat blue cheese in place of the feta
and chopped tomatoes in place of the onion.

Smothered Triple-Onion Brisket Sandwiches

Makes 1 pound 2 ounces cooked beef and 2 cups onion sauce
Serves: 8
Serving Size: about 2 1/4 ounces cooked beef, 1/4 cup onion sauce, 1 1/2 ounces bread

Exchanges/ Food Choices:
2 Starch
4 Lean Meat

Calories	350
Calories from Fat	60
Total Fat	6g
Saturated Fat	1.5g
Trans Fat	0g
Monounsaturated Fat	1.5g
Cholesterol	75mg
Sodium	590mg
Potassium	701mg
Total Carbohydrate	35g
Dietary Fiber	9g
Sugars	9g
Protein	33g

Nonstick cooking spray

2 cups diced onion

2 pounds lean beef brisket, trimmed of fat

1 cup dry red wine **or** 3/4 cup water and 2 tablespoons balsamic vinegar

2 teaspoons Worcestershire sauce

2 tablespoons dried minced onion

1 tablespoon sodium-free beef bouillon granules

1 1/2 teaspoons instant coffee granules, preferably espresso variety

1 1/2 teaspoons dried oregano leaves

1 teaspoon onion powder

1 teaspoon garlic powder

3/4 teaspoon salt

16-ounce loaf whole-grain Italian bread, cut into 16 slices

1 **Coat a 6-quart slow cooker with cooking spray.** Place the onions on the bottom of the slow cooker.

2 **Heat a large nonstick skillet over medium-high heat.** Brown the beef 3 minutes on each side.

3 **Place beef on top of the onions.** Pour the wine and Worcestershire sauce over all. Sprinkle with the remaining ingredients, except the salt and bread. Cover and cook on low only for 5 1/2 hours or until tender.

4 **Remove the beef from the slow cooker, turning several times to keep topping in the slow cooker.** Place beef on cutting board and let stand 15 minutes before thinly slicing against the grain. Stir the salt into the onion mixture. Place the beef on bread slices and spoon the onion sauce on top.

Veggie-Packed, Very Sloppy Joes

Makes about 3 1/3 cups beef mixture
Serves: 6
Serving Size: about 1/2 cup beef mixture plus 1 bun

Exchanges/ Food Choices:
2 Starch
1 Vegetable
2 Lean Meat

Calories	260
Calories from Fat	45
Total Fat	5g
Saturated Fat	1g
Trans Fat	0g
Monounsaturated Fat	1.5g
Cholesterol	30mg
Sodium	540mg
Potassium	512mg
Total Carbohydrate	39g
Dietary Fiber	6g
Sugars	13g
Protein	17g

Nonstick cooking spray

12 ounces extra-lean ground beef

1 cup diced onion

1 cup diced red or yellow bell pepper

1 medium zucchini or yellow squash, halved lengthwise and thinly sliced

3 ounces no-salt-added tomato paste

1/4 cup water

2 tablespoons sugar

2 tablespoons cider vinegar

1 tablespoon Worcestershire sauce

3/4 teaspoon ground cumin

3/4 teaspoon salt

1 cup frozen corn kernels

6 whole-wheat hamburger buns, lightly toasted

1 Lightly coat a 3 1/2- to 4-quart slow cooker with cooking spray.

2 **Heat a medium nonstick skillet over medium-high heat.** Brown the beef, about 2 minutes, stirring frequently.

3 **Place in the slow cooker with the remaining ingredients, except the corn and buns.** Stir until well blended. Cover and cook on high for 3 hours, or on low for 6 hours, or until squash is very tender.

4 **Stir in the corn, cover, and let stand 15 minutes to absorb flavors and warm corn.**

5 **Serve as open-face sandwiches over lightly toasted whole-wheat hamburger buns.**

Cook's Note:
The squash breaks down and "disappears" and acts as a thickener. Omit buns, if desired, and serve over 1/2 cup cooked brown rice or whole-grain elbow macaroni per serving.

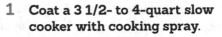

Taco Night Filling

Makes 5 cups
Serves: 10
Serving Size: 1/2 cup

**Exchanges/
Food Choices:**
1 Vegetable
2 Lean Meat

Calories	110
Calories from Fat	25
Total Fat	3g
Saturated Fat	1g
Trans Fat	0g
Monounsaturated Fat	1g
Cholesterol	35mg
Sodium	170mg
Potassium	81mg
Total Carbohydrate	7g
Dietary Fiber	1g
Sugars	4g
Protein	14g

Nonstick cooking spray

1 1/2 pounds extra-lean ground beef

1 1/2 cups diced onion

1 cup grape tomatoes, halved

8-ounce can no-salt-added tomato sauce

2 tablespoons smoked paprika

1 tablespoon ground cumin

2–3 teaspoons sugar

2 teaspoons sodium-free beef bouillon granules

1 1/2 teaspoons onion powder

1/2 teaspoon garlic powder

1/8 teaspoon cayenne, *optional*

1/2 teaspoon salt

1 **Coat a 3 1/2- to 4-quart slow cooker with cooking spray.**

2 **Heat a large nonstick skillet over medium-high heat.** Working in two batches, brown the beef for 3–4 minutes, stirring frequently.

3 **Place the beef in the slow cooker with the remaining ingredients, except the salt.** Cover and cook on high for 3 hours or on low for 6 hours. Stir in the salt.

Cook's Note:
Freezes well. May serve on one fat-free whole-wheat tortilla, over 1/2 cup whole-grain rotini, or over 2 cups salad greens per serving.

Pork-Cilantro Tortillas

Makes 2 cups pork mixture
Serves: 6
Serving Size: 1 filled tortilla

Exchanges/ Food Choices:
2 Starch
2 Lean Meat
1/2 Fat

Calories	270
Calories from Fat	60
Total Fat	6g
Saturated Fat	1g
Trans Fat	0g
Monounsaturated Fat	2g
Cholesterol	50mg
Sodium	650mg
Potassium	478mg
Total Carbohydrate	33g
Dietary Fiber	5g
Sugars	7g
Protein	21g

FILLING
Nonstick cooking spray

1 1/2 teaspoons chili powder

1 teaspoon ground cumin

1/2 teaspoon salt

1/4 teaspoon black pepper

1 pound pork tenderloin

1/4 cup water

1 tablespoon extra-virgin olive oil

4 medium garlic cloves, peeled

6 8-inch whole-wheat tortillas, warmed

TOPPING
1/4 cup honey mustard

2 tablespoons fat-free milk or water

6 cups shredded romaine lettuce

1/2 cup thinly sliced or diced red onion

1/2 cup chopped cilantro leaves

1 medium lime, cut into 6 wedges

1 **Lightly coat a 3 1/2- to 4-quart slow cooker with cooking spray.**

2 **In a small bowl, combine the chili powder, cumin, salt, and pepper.** Coat the pork with the mixture.

3 **Place the water, oil, and garlic cloves in the slow cooker and stir.** Place the pork on top of the garlic cloves. Cover and cook on high for 1 hour and 25 minutes, or on low for 2 hours and 45 minutes, or until the internal temperature of the pork reaches 145°F.

4 **Place pork on cutting board and let stand 5 minutes before thinly slicing.** Whisk the pan drippings to break down garlic. Return the pork to the pan drippings and stir. Serve equal amounts of the pork, about 1/3 cup, on each tortilla.

5 **In a small bowl, stir together the honey mustard and milk.** Top pork with lettuce, honey mustard mixture, onions, and cilantro. Serve with lime wedges to squeeze over all.

Sweet Smoky Pork Tortillas

Makes 4 cups pork mixture
Serves: 8
Serving Size: 1/2 cup pork mixture, 1 tortilla, 1/2 cup lettuce, and 2 tablespoons sour cream

Exchanges/ Food Choices:
2 Starch
1 Vegetable
2 Lean Meat
1 1/2 Fat

Calories	340
Calories from Fat	100
Total Fat	12g
Saturated Fat	3g
Trans Fat	0g
Monounsaturated Fat	4g
Cholesterol	35mg
Sodium	470mg
Potassium	442mg
Total Carbohydrate	37g
Dietary Fiber	5g
Sugars	10g
Protein	18g

Nonstick cooking spray

2 cups diced onion

1 cup diced green bell pepper

14.5-ounce can no-salt-added stewed tomatoes, drained

1 pound boneless pork chops, trimmed of fat

1 teaspoon smoked paprika

1/4 cup chopped cilantro leaves

1/4 cup ketchup

1 tablespoon extra-virgin olive oil

1 teaspoon ground cumin

1/2 teaspoon salt

8 8-inch fat-free whole-wheat flour tortillas

4 cups shredded romaine lettuce

1 cup fat-free sour cream

1 **Coat a 3 1/2- to 4-quart slow cooker with cooking spray.** Add the onions, bell pepper, and tomatoes in the slow cooker, top with the pork, and sprinkle evenly with the paprika. Cover and cook on high for 4 hours, or on low for 8 hours, or until pork shreds easily with a fork.

2 **Remove pork and shred with a fork.** Return to the slow cooker with the cilantro, ketchup, oil, cumin, and salt. Stir until well blended.

3 **Warm tortillas according to package directions.** Spoon 1/2 cup pork mixture on top of each tortilla and top each with 1/2 cup lettuce and 2 tablespoons sour cream.

Tangy Sweet BBQ Pork

Makes 4 cups
Serves: 8
Serving Size: 1/2 cup

**Exchanges/
Food Choices:**
1/2 Carbohydrate
2 Lean Meat
1 Fat

Calories	160
Calories from Fat	80
Total Fat	9g
Saturated Fat	1.5g
Trans Fat	0g
Monounsaturated Fat	3.5g
Cholesterol	45mg
Sodium	390mg
Potassium	233mg
Total Carbohydrate	6g
Dietary Fiber	1g
Sugars	1g
Protein	14g

Nonstick cooking spray

1 1/2 cups diced onion

1 1/2 pounds boneless pork chops, trimmed of fat

2 tablespoons canola oil

1 1/2 teaspoons ground cumin

1/2 teaspoon ground cinnamon

1/4 teaspoon ground allspice

1 cup low-sodium hickory or mesquite barbecue sauce

1 tablespoon cider vinegar

1 tablespoon prepared mustard

2 teaspoons liquid smoke

1. **Coat a 3 1/2- to 4-quart slow cooker with cooking spray.** Place onions on bottom of the slow cooker and arrange the pork chops on top of the onions, overlapping slightly. Drizzle the oil evenly over all.

2. **In a small bowl, combine the cumin, cinnamon, and allspice and sprinkle evenly over the pork chops.** Cover and cook on high for 4 hours or on low for 8 hours.

3. **Using two forks, shred the pork in the slow cooker.** Stir in the remaining ingredients. Cover and cook on high for 30 minutes to allow the flavors to absorb.

Cook's Note:
May serve on whole-wheat hamburger buns, on top of baked potatoes, or on romaine lettuce as a healthy wrap.

No-Fried "Refried" Black Beans

Makes 2 cups
Serves: 6
Serving Size: 1/3 cup

**Exchanges/
Food Choices:**
1 Starch
1 Lean Meat

Calories	140
Calories from Fat	30
Total Fat	3.5g
Saturated Fat	0.5g
Trans Fat	0g
Monounsaturated Fat	2.5g
Cholesterol	0mg
Sodium	310mg
Potassium	465mg
Total Carbohydrate	21g
Dietary Fiber	7g
Sugars	5g
Protein	6g

1 cup dried black beans

6 cups water, divided

Nonstick cooking spray

1 cup diced onion

1 medium jalapeño pepper, stemmed and halved lengthwise

3 whole garlic cloves, peeled

1 1/2 tablespoons extra-virgin olive oil

3/4 teaspoon salt

1 **Place beans and 4 cups water in a bowl.** Cover and soak overnight or place in a large saucepan, bring to a boil over high heat, and boil for 2 minutes. Remove from heat, cover, and let stand 1 hour. Drain beans in a colander and rinse well. Shake off excess liquid.

2 **Coat a 3 1/2- to 4-quart slow cooker with cooking spray.** Place the drained beans, the remaining 2 cups water, onion, jalapeño, and garlic in the slow cooker. Cover and cook on high for 4 hours, or on low for 8 hours, or until tender.

3 **Place a colander over a medium bowl.** Drain the beans, reserving the liquid. Roughly mash the beans with a potato masher or an electric mixer on low. Stir in the oil, salt, and 2–3 tablespoons reserved liquid. For a thinner consistency, add 2–3 additional tablespoons liquid.

Cook's Note:
May use as a dip, a side dish, or a filler for meatless tacos!

White Bean Crostini

Makes 2 cups bean mixture
Serves: 4
Serving Size: 1/2 cup bean mixture and 8 bread slices

**Exchanges/
Food Choices:**
2 Starch
1 Vegetable
1 Lean Meat
2 1/2 Fat

Calories	350
Calories from Fat	140
Total Fat	16g
Saturated Fat	2g
Trans Fat	0g
Monounsaturated Fat	7g
Cholesterol	0mg
Sodium	570mg
Potassium	326mg
Total Carbohydrate	40g
Dietary Fiber	6g
Sugars	5g
Protein	12g

Nonstick cooking spray

1 cup diced onion

1 large yellow or green bell pepper, cut into 1/2-inch pieces

1/4 cup pine nuts

2 tablespoons extra-virgin olive oil, divided

6 ounces whole-grain baguette bread, cut in 32 thin slices

1/2 15-ounce can no-salt-added Great Northern beans or other white bean, rinsed and drained

2 medium plum tomatoes, chopped

1 medium garlic clove, halved crosswise

1 1/2 teaspoons cider vinegar

16 pitted kalamata olives, coarsely chopped

1/2 cup crumbled fat-free feta cheese

1/4 cup chopped fresh basil

1 **Coat a 6-quart slow cooker with cooking spray.** Place the onions, peppers, pine nuts, and 1 tablespoon oil in the slow cooker. Toss to coat well. Cover and cook on high for 2 1/2 hours, or on low for 5 hours, or until vegetables are tender.

2 **Put the bread slices on a large baking sheet and place in the oven.** Turn oven to 350°F. Bake the bread for 8 minutes or until lightly browned on the bottom. Remove from oven and cool.

3 **When vegetables are cooked, stir in the beans, tomatoes, garlic, and vinegar.** Cover and cook 15 minutes on high. Gently stir in the olives and remaining 1 tablespoon oil. Spoon equal amounts of the vegetable mixture, about 1 tablespoon, on each bread slice and sprinkle evenly with the feta and basil.

Cook's Note:

There is no need to wait for the oven to preheat when toasting the baguette. Just put the slices in and wait for perfectly toasted bread!

Lima Bean Hummus Pile Ups

Makes 1 1/2 cups hummus
Serves: 6
Serving Size: 1/4 cup hummus, 1 cheese slice, and 8 crackers

Exchanges/ Food Choices:
2 1/2 Starch
1 Medium-Fat Meat
1 Fat

Calories	320
Calories from Fat	100
Total Fat	11g
Saturated Fat	3g
Trans Fat	0g
Monounsaturated Fat	3.5g
Cholesterol	10mg
Sodium	540mg
Potassium	181mg
Total Carbohydrate	42g
Dietary Fiber	8g
Sugars	1g
Protein	16g

Nonstick cooking spray

2 cups frozen lima beans

1/2 cup water

3 medium garlic cloves, peeled

1/4 teaspoon salt

1/4 cup chopped fresh parsley

1/4 cup slivered almonds

1–1 1/2 tablespoons lemon juice

1 tablespoon extra-virgin olive oil

6 thin slices reduced-fat Swiss cheese, cut into 8 pieces each

48 fat-free wheat crackers

1 **Coat a 3 1/2- to 4-quart slow cooker with cooking spray.** Place the beans, water, garlic, and salt in the slow cooker. Cover and cook on high for 1 1/2 hours, or on low for 3 hours, or until beans are tender.

2 **Place bean mixture in blender with the parsley, almonds, lemon juice, and oil.** Purée until smooth.

3 **Serve warm or chilled on top of the cheese and crackers.**

Eggplant-Garbanzo Lettuce Wraps

Makes 3 cups garbanzo mixture
Serves: 4
Serving Size: 3/4 cup garbanzo mixture, 3 lettuce leaves, and 3 tablespoons yogurt

Exchanges/ Food Choices:
2 Carbohydrate
1 Lean Meat
2 Fat

Calories	280
Calories from Fat	100
Total Fat	12g
Saturated Fat	1g
Trans Fat	0g
Monounsaturated Fat	6.5g
Cholesterol	0mg
Sodium	340mg
Potassium	636mg
Total Carbohydrate	35g
Dietary Fiber	9g
Sugars	17g
Protein	12g

Nonstick cooking spray

1 cup diced onion

1 cup diced red bell pepper

1/4 cup golden raisins

1/2 16-ounce can no-salt-added garbanzo beans

2 tablespoons no-salt-added tomato paste

2 tablespoons water

1 teaspoon apple pie spice

1/2 teaspoon ground cumin

1 tablespoon canola oil

8 ounces eggplant, cut into 1/2-inch cubes

2 ounces (1/2 cup) slivered almonds, toasted

1/2 teaspoon salt

12 large romaine lettuce leaves

3/4 cup fat-free plain Greek yogurt

1 **Coat a 3 1/2- to 4-quart slow cooker with cooking spray.** Stir together the onions, bell pepper, raisins, garbanzo beans, tomato paste, water, apple pie spice, and cumin in the slow cooker.

2 **Heat the oil in a large nonstick skillet over medium-high heat.** Brown the eggplant 3 minutes, stirring occasionally. Add to the slow cooker. Stir, cover, and cook on high for 2 hours, or on low for 4 hours, or until vegetables are tender.

3 **Turn off the heat, stir in the almonds and salt.** Let stand, uncovered, for 15 minutes to absorb flavors. Serve in lettuce leaves and top with the yogurt.

CHAPTER 4
Soups and Chilis

Hearty Chicken Chipotle Soup with Hominy

Herbed Parmesan Chicken Soup

Chicken Salsa Verde Chili

Good "Cents" Gumbo

Italian Chicken Sausage-Potato Soup

Hearty Turkey Sausage and Wild Rice Soup

Italian Kidney Bean Soup

Chop-Free Chili

Grandma's Vegetable Beef Soup

Beer-Bottle Chili

Clam and Sausage Chowder

Tilapia-Tomato Chowder

Spicy Shrimp, Spicy Thai Soup

Lentil-Ginger Soup

Chunky Italian Garden Veggie Soup

Fresh Fennel Bean Soup with Parmesan

Gingered Pumpkin Bisque

Hearty Chicken Chipotle Soup with Hominy

Makes 8 cups
Serves: 8
Serving Size: 1 cup

**Exchanges/
Food Choices:**
1/2 Starch
2 Vegetable
1 Lean Meat
1 Fat

Calories	190
Calories from Fat	60
Total Fat	7g
Saturated Fat	1.5g
Trans Fat	0g
Monounsaturated Fat	3g
Cholesterol	35mg
Sodium	390mg
Potassium	356mg
Total Carbohydrate	18g
Dietary Fiber	4g
Sugars	7g
Protein	13g

Nonstick cooking spray

1 pound boneless, skinless, chicken thigh meat, trimmed of fat and cut into bite-size pieces

1 cup diced onion

2 cups reduced-sodium chicken broth, divided

2 cups diced red bell pepper

14.5-ounce can no-salt-added stewed tomatoes

15.5-ounce can yellow hominy, rinsed and drained

1–2 chipotle chili peppers (canned in adobo sauce), mashed and finely chopped

1 tablespoon sugar

1 1/2 teaspoons ground cumin

1 tablespoon extra-virgin olive oil

3/4 teaspoon salt

1 Lightly coat a 3 1/2- to 4-quart slow cooker with cooking spray.

2 Lightly coat a large skillet with cooking spray and place over medium-high heat until hot. Working in batches, brown the chicken. Remove the chicken with a slotted spoon and place in the slow cooker.

3 To pan drippings, add the onion and cook until tender, about 3 minutes. Add to the slow cooker.

4 Pour 1 cup broth into the skillet and scrape bottom and sides to remove any brown bits. Pour into the slow cooker with the remaining ingredients, except the oil and salt. Cover and cook on high for 3 hours, or on low for 6 hours, or until onions are tender. Stir in the oil and salt.

Cook's Note:
Flavors are even better the next day.

Herbed Parmesan Chicken Soup

Makes 10 cups
Serves: 10
Serving Size: 1 cup soup
plus 1 tablespoon cheese

**Exchanges/
Food Choices:**
2 Vegetable
2 Lean Meat
1 Fat

Calories	190
Calories from Fat	80
Total Fat	8g
Saturated Fat	2.5g
Trans Fat	0g
Monounsaturated Fat	2.5g
Cholesterol	50mg
Sodium	300mg
Potassium	312mg
Total Carbohydrate	12g
Dietary Fiber	3g
Sugars	5g
Protein	17g

Nonstick cooking spray

1 pound boneless, skinless, chicken thigh meat, trimmed of fat and cut into bite-size pieces

1 1/2 cups diced onion

2 medium carrots, peeled and sliced

2 14.5-ounce cans no-salt-added stewed tomatoes

14.5-ounce can fat-free, reduced-sodium chicken broth

1 tablespoon dried basil leaves

1 teaspoon dried oregano leaves

1/2 teaspoon dried rosemary leaves

1/4 teaspoon dried red pepper flakes

2 ounces uncooked whole-grain rotini

1 tablespoon extra-virgin olive oil

1/2 teaspoon salt

2/3 cup grated Parmesan cheese

1 **Coat a 3 1/2- to 4-quart slow cooker with cooking spray.**

2 **Place the chicken, onion, carrots, tomatoes, broth, basil, oregano, rosemary, and pepper flakes in the slow cooker.** Cover and cook on high for 4 hours, or on low for 7–8 hours, or until vegetables are tender.

3 **Stir in the pasta.** Cover and cook 15 minutes on high or 25–30 minutes on low. Stir in the oil and salt. Top each serving with 1 tablespoon Parmesan cheese.

Chicken Salsa Verde Chili

Makes 4 cups
Serves: 4
Serving Size: 1 cup chili,
2 tablespoons sour cream,
and 1 tablespoon cilantro

**Exchanges/
Food Choices:**
1 Starch
1 Vegetable
3 Lean Meat
2 1/2 Fat

Calories	350
Calories from Fat	150
Total Fat	17g
Saturated Fat	3.5g
Trans Fat	0g
Monounsaturated Fat	8g
Cholesterol	75mg
Sodium	520mg
Potassium	578mg
Total Carbohydrate	22g
Dietary Fiber	4g
Sugars	8g
Protein	26g

Nonstick cooking spray

1 pound boneless, skinless, chicken thighs, trimmed of fat and cut into 1-inch pieces

1 teaspoon ground cumin, preferably roasted

8-ounce can salsa verde

1/2 16-ounce package frozen stir-fry vegetables, thawed

1/2 15-ounce can no-salt-added navy beans, rinsed and drained

5 ounces (1 cup) grape tomatoes, quartered

2 tablespoons extra-virgin olive oil

1/2 cup fat-free sour cream

1/4 cup chopped fresh cilantro leaves

1 **Heat a large skillet coated with cooking spray over medium-high heat.** Add the chicken and sprinkle evenly with the cumin. Brown chicken pieces, stirring occasionally.

2 **Coat a 3 1/2- to 4-quart slow cooker with cooking spray.** Add the chicken, salsa, stir-fry vegetables, beans, and tomatoes. Cover and cook on high for 3 hours, or on low for 5 1/2–6 hours, or until vegetables are tender. Stir in the oil.

3 **Serve in bowls topped with sour cream and cilantro.**

Cook's Note:
This recipe may be doubled easily, if desired.

Good "Cents" Gumbo

**Makes 6 cups gumbo
and 2 cups cooked rice**
Serves: 6
Serving Size: 1 cup gumbo
and 1/3 cup cooked rice

**Exchanges/
Food Choices:**
1 Starch
1 Vegetable
2 Lean Meat
1 1/2 Fat

Calories	280
Calories from Fat	100
Total Fat	12g
Saturated Fat	2.5g
Trans Fat	0g
Monounsaturated Fat	5.5g
Cholesterol	55mg
Sodium	560mg
Potassium	433mg
Total Carbohydrate	18g
Dietary Fiber	3g
Sugars	2g
Protein	24g

Nonstick cooking spray

1 pound bag frozen
   pepper stir-fry

2 medium celery stalks,
   sliced

2 cups (1 pint) grape
   tomatoes

2 teaspoons no-salt-
   added seafood
   seasoning or no-salt-
   added Creole or Cajun
   seasoning

8 ounces boneless,
   skinless, chicken thigh
   meat, trimmed of fat
   and cut into bite-size
   pieces

2 tablespoons extra-
   virgin olive oil, divided

8 ounces smoked turkey
   sausage, thinly sliced

8 ounces raw shrimp,
   peeled

1/2 cup water

10-ounce bag frozen
   brown rice

1 tablespoon Louisiana
   hot sauce or to taste

1/2 teaspoon salt

1 **Lightly coat a 3 1/2- to 4-quart
slow cooker with cooking spray.**
Add the pepper stir-fry, celery,
tomatoes, seasoning, and thigh
meat to the slow cooker. Cover and
cook on low for 7 hours, or on high
for 3 1/2 hours, or until celery is
very tender.

2 **Heat 1 teaspoon oil in a large
nonstick skillet over medium-high
heat.** Brown the sausage, about
3 minutes, stirring occasionally. Stir
the sausage into the slow cooker
with the shrimp. Add the water
to the skillet, scraping to remove
any browned bits. Add to the slow
cooker. Cover and cook on high for
30 minutes.

3 **After 30 minutes, stir in the
remaining oil, hot sauce, and
salt, breaking up the tomatoes
while stirring.** At time of serving,
cook rice according to package
directions and serve gumbo over
rice.

Cook's Note:
The whole tomatoes will pop as you stir them at the end, just as whole cranberries
do! Flavors will improve overnight. No-salt-added seafood seasoning and no-salt-
added Creole or Cajun seasonings may be purchased at health food stores.

CHILIS SOUPS CHI SOUPS CHIL CHILIS SOUPS CHILIS SOUPS CHILIS SOUPS CHILIS SOUPS CHILIS SOUPS CHILIS SOUPS CHILIS SOUPS SOUPS CHILIS SOUPS CHILIS

SOUPS

Italian Chicken Sausage-Potato Soup

Makes about 6 cups
Serves: 6
Serving Size: about 1 cup

Exchanges/ Food Choices:
1 Starch
2 Vegetable
1 Lean Meat

Calories	210
Calories from Fat	80
Total Fat	9g
Saturated Fat	2.5g
Trans Fat	0g
Monounsaturated Fat	0g
Cholesterol	25mg
Sodium	480mg
Potassium	702mg
Total Carbohydrate	25g
Dietary Fiber	4g
Sugars	5g
Protein	8g

Nonstick cooking spray

1 1/4 pounds baking potatoes, unpeeled and cut into 1/2-inch cubes

2 cups matchstick carrots

1 1/2 cups diced onion

2 medium celery stalks, thinly sliced

2 14.5-ounce cans fat-free, reduced-sodium chicken broth

1 teaspoon dried thyme leaves

2 dried bay leaves

1/2 teaspoon black pepper

7 ounces low-sodium hot Italian chicken sausage, casings removed

1/4 cup chopped fresh parsley, *optional*

1 **Coat a 3 1/2- to 4-quart slow cooker with cooking spray.** Combine the potatoes, carrots, onions, celery, broth, thyme, bay leaves, and black pepper in the slow cooker. Cover and cook on high for 3 hours, or on low for 5 1/2–6 hours, or until vegetables are tender.

2 **Thirty minutes before serving, heat a large skillet coated with cooking spray over medium-high heat.** Cook the sausage, breaking up larger pieces while cooking.

3 **Working with 1 cup at a time, purée 3 cups vegetables in a blender.** After the vegetables have been puréed, return them to the slow cooker with the sausage. Cover, turn off the heat, and let stand 15 minutes to allow flavors to blend. Sprinkle with parsley, if desired.

Hearty Turkey Sausage and Wild Rice Soup

Makes 6 cups
Serves: 6
Serving Size: 1 cup

**Exchanges/
Food Choices:**
1 1/2 Starch
1 Vegetable
1 Medium-Fat Meat

Calories	210
Calories from Fat	35
Total Fat	4g
Saturated Fat	0g
Trans Fat	0g
Monounsaturated Fat	0g
Cholesterol	20mg
Sodium	590mg
Potassium	718mg
Total Carbohydrate	31g
Dietary Fiber	6g
Sugars	5g
Protein	13g

Nonstick cooking spray

8 ounces hot Italian turkey sausage, casings removed

1 1/2 cups diced onion

1 cup sliced carrots

1 cup diced celery

3 ounces uncooked wild rice

3 cups hot water

15-ounce can no-salt-added navy beans, rinsed and drained

1 tablespoon sodium-free beef bouillon granules

1 teaspoon dried thyme leaves

1/2 teaspoon dried sage

1/2 teaspoon salt

1/2 cup chopped fresh parsley

1   Coat a 3 1/2- to 4-quart slow cooker with cooking spray.

2   **Heat a large skillet coated with cooking spray over medium-high heat.** Brown the sausage 3–4 minutes, breaking up large pieces. Place in the slow cooker with the remaining ingredients, except the parsley. Cover and cook on high for 2 1/2 hours or on low for 5 hours.

3   **Stir in the parsley and serve.**

Italian Kidney Bean Soup

Makes 6 cups
Serves: 6
Serving Size: 1 cup soup,
1 tablespoon mozzarella,
and 1 teaspoon Parmesan

**Exchanges/
Food Choices:**
1 Starch
1 Vegetable
1 Medium-Fat Meat

Calories	230
Calories from Fat	90
Total Fat	10g
Saturated Fat	3.5g
Trans Fat	0g
Monounsaturated Fat	0g
Cholesterol	25mg
Sodium	530mg
Potassium	395mg
Total Carbohydrate	22g
Dietary Fiber	6g
Sugars	5g
Protein	13g

Nonstick cooking spray

6 ounces low-sodium hot
Italian turkey sausage,
casings removed

12 ounces frozen pepper
stir-fry, thawed

2 cups diced eggplant

15-ounce can no-salt-
added dark kidney
beans, rinsed and
drained

14.5-ounce can no-salt-
added diced tomatoes

1 tablespoon sodium-free
beef bouillon granules

1 tablespoon chili powder

1 teaspoon garlic powder

1/4 teaspoon dried pepper
flakes, *optional*

1/4–1/2 teaspoon dried
fennel seed

1/4 teaspoon salt

1 1/2 ounces (1/3 cup)
part-skim mozzarella
cheese, shredded

2 tablespoons grated
Parmesan cheese

1 **Coat a 3 1/2- to 4-quart slow
cooker with cooking spray.**

2 **Heat a medium skillet, coated
with cooking spray, over medium-
high heat.** Brown the sausage, 3–4
minutes, breaking up large pieces.
Place in the slow cooker with the
remaining ingredients, except the
cheeses. Cover and cook on high for
4 hours or on low for 8 hours.

3 **Serve topped with mozzarella and
Parmesan.**

Cook's Note:
Even better the next day. Recipe freezes well without the
cheese.

Chop-Free Chili

Makes 7 cups
Serves: 7
Serving Size: 1 cup

**Exchanges/
Food Choices:**
1 Starch
2 Vegetable
2 Lean Meat
1 Fat

Calories	340
Calories from Fat	100
Total Fat	12g
Saturated Fat	2.5g
Trans Fat	0g
Monounsaturated Fat	0.5g
Cholesterol	60mg
Sodium	790mg
Potassium	273mg
Total Carbohydrate	32g
Dietary Fiber	9g
Sugars	9g
Protein	26g

Nonstick cooking spray

12 ounces extra-lean ground beef

3 1/2 ounces sweet Italian turkey breakfast sausage links, casings removed

15-ounce can no-salt-added pinto or kidney beans, rinsed and drained

8 ounces frozen pepper stir-fry

2 14.5-ounce cans no-salt-added stewed tomatoes

2 teaspoons sugar

1 tablespoon chili powder

1 tablespoon ground cumin, divided

2 ounces baked tortilla chips, coarsely crushed

2 ounces (1/2 cup) reduced-fat sharp Cheddar cheese, shredded

1/4 teaspoon salt

1 **Lightly coat a 3 1/2- to 4-quart slow cooker with cooking spray.**

2 **Lightly coat a large skillet with cooking spray and place over medium-high heat until hot.** Brown the beef and sausage, about 2 minutes, stirring frequently.

3 **Place in the slow cooker and stir in the beans, pepper stir-fry, tomatoes, sugar, chili powder, and 2 teaspoons cumin.** Cover and cook on high for 3 1/2 hours or on low for 7 hours.

4 **Stir in the remaining ingredients.** Cover and let stand on low for 15 minutes to absorb flavors. Flavor improves overnight.

CHILIS SOUPS CH

SOUPS

CHILIS SOUPS CHIL

CHILIS SOUPS CHILIS SOUPS CHILIS SOUPS CHILIS SOUPS CHILIS SOUPS CHILIS SOUPS CHILIS **SOUPS** CHILIS SOUPS CHILIS SOUPS

Grandma's Vegetable Beef Soup

Makes 9 cups
Serves: 9
Serving Size: 1 cup

**Exchanges/
Food Choices:**
3 Vegetable
2 Lean Meat
1 Fat

Calories	200
Calories from Fat	60
Total Fat	7g
Saturated Fat	1.5g
Trans Fat	0g
Monounsaturated Fat	3.5g
Cholesterol	50mg
Sodium	490mg
Potassium	566mg
Total Carbohydrate	15g
Dietary Fiber	3g
Sugars	8g
Protein	20g

*FIX-IT & FORGET-IT
LIGHTLY
Pg. 161
DAWN's Quick & HEALTHY
Veg Soup*

Nonstick cooking spray

2 tablespoons extra-virgin olive oil, divided

1 pound trimmed extra-lean beef chuck roast, cut into bite-size pieces

2 cups water, divided

2 cups frozen cut green beans, thawed

1 1/2 cups sliced fresh or frozen carrots, thawed

12-ounce package frozen pepper stir-fry, thawed

14.5-ounce can no-salt-added stewed tomatoes

1 tablespoon sodium-free beef bouillon granules

2 teaspoons instant coffee granules, *optional*

2 teaspoons dried oregano leaves.

1/2 cup ketchup, divided

1 teaspoon salt

3 cups coarsely chopped green cabbage

1   Coat a 5- to 6-quart slow cooker with cooking spray.

2   **Heat 1 tablespoon oil in a large skillet over medium-high heat and brown the beef for about 5 minutes, stirring occasionally.** Place in slow cooker.

3   **Add 1/2 cup water to the skillet to deglaze, scraping bottom and sides, and add to the slow cooker with the remaining water, beans, carrots, pepper stir-fry, tomatoes, bouillon granules, coffee granules, oregano, and 1/4 cup ketchup.** Cover and cook on high for 4 1/2 hours, or on low for 8–9 hours, or until beef is tender.

4   **Stir in the remaining ingredients, cover, and cook 30 minutes or until cabbage is tender.**

↓ *Pg. 14*

Cook's Note:
This recipe tastes even better the next day.

Beer-Bottle Chili

Makes 8 cups
Serves: 8
Serving Size: 1 cup chili and
1 tablespoon sour cream

**Exchanges/
Food Choices:**
1 Starch
1 Vegetable
2 Lean Meat

Calories	190
Calories from Fat	25
Total Fat	3g
Saturated Fat	1g
Trans Fat	0g
Monounsaturated Fat	1g
Cholesterol	30mg
Sodium	430mg
Potassium	314mg
Total Carbohydrate	22g
Dietary Fiber	4g
Sugars	5g
Protein	16g

Nonstick cooking spray

1 pound extra-lean ground beef or turkey

1 3/4-ounce package chili seasoning mix

12 ounces light beer

2 14.5-ounce cans no-salt-added stewed tomatoes

15-ounce can no-salt-added pinto or dark kidney beans, rinsed and drained

8 ounces frozen pepper stir-fry, thawed

1/2 teaspoon salt

1/2 cup fat-free sour cream

1 **Coat a 3 1/2- to 4-quart slow cooker with cooking spray.**

2 **Heat a large skillet coated with cooking spray over medium-high heat.** Brown the ground beef for 3–4 minutes, stirring frequently. Place in the slow cooker with the remaining ingredients, except the sour cream. Cover and cook on high for 4 hours or on low for 8 hours.

3 **Serve topped with sour cream.**

Cook's Note:
Even better the next day. Freezes well.

Clam and Sausage Chowder

Makes 6 cups
Serves: 6
Serving Size: 1 cup

**Exchanges/
Food Choices:**
1/2 Starch
1/2 Fat-Free Milk
1 Vegetable
1/2 Fat

Calories	140
Calories from Fat	35
Total Fat	4g
Saturated Fat	1g
Trans Fat	0g
Monounsaturated Fat	1g
Cholesterol	20mg
Sodium	460mg
Potassium	439mg
Total Carbohydrate	17g
Dietary Fiber	2g
Sugars	8g
Protein	10g

Nonstick cooking spray

4 ounces smoked turkey sausage, diced

1 cup water, divided

1 1/2 cups diced onion

8 ounces diced potatoes

1/2 cup diced celery

2 medium garlic cloves, minced

1/2 teaspoon dried thyme leaves

1 dried bay leaf

1/2 teaspoon black pepper

2 1/2 cups fat-free milk

6.5-ounce can minced clams, rinsed and drained

2 tablespoons trans-fat-free margarine

1 Coat a 3 1/2- to 4-quart slow cooker with cooking spray.

2 **Heat a medium skillet coated with cooking spray over medium-high heat.** Brown the sausage for 3–4 minutes, stirring frequently. Place in a small bowl, cover, and refrigerate until needed.

3 **To pan residue, add 1/2 cup water and scrape bottom and sides to release any browned bits.** Place in the slow cooker with the remaining water, onions, potatoes, celery, garlic, thyme, bay leaf, and black pepper. Cover and cook for 2 1/2 hours on high, or on low for 5 hours, or until onions are tender.

4 **Working in 1-cup batches, purée 2 cups potato mixture in a blender, being sure to secure the lid tightly while puréeing.** Return the mixture to the slow cooker, stir in the sausage and the remaining ingredients. Cover and cook on high for 30 minutes.

Cook's Note:
Even better the next day.

Tilapia-Tomato Chowder

Makes 8 cups
Serves: 8
Serving Size: 1 cup

**Exchanges/
Food Choices:**
1/2 Starch
1 Vegetable
1 Lean Meat
1 1/2 Fat

Calories	180
Calories from Fat	70
Total Fat	8g
Saturated Fat	1.5g
Trans Fat	0g
Monounsaturated Fat	3.5g
Cholesterol	30mg
Sodium	370mg
Potassium	483mg
Total Carbohydrate	16g
Dietary Fiber	2g
Sugars	4g
Protein	14g

Nonstick cooking spray

4 ounces smoked turkey sausage, diced

14-ounce can reduced-sodium chicken broth, divided

14.5-ounce can no-salt-added diced tomatoes

12 ounces red or Yukon gold potatoes, scrubbed and diced

1 cup diced red onion

1 cup frozen corn kernels, thawed

1 1/2 teaspoons seafood seasoning, such as Old Bay

1 teaspoon dried oregano leaves

1/2 teaspoon dried thyme leaves

12 ounces tilapia fillets or other lean white fish, cut into 1-inch pieces

1/2 cup chopped fresh parsley

2 tablespoons extra-virgin olive oil

2 tablespoons trans-fat-free margarine

1/2 teaspoon salt

1 **Coat a 3 1/2- to 4-quart slow cooker with cooking spray.**

2 **Heat a medium skillet coated with cooking spray over medium-high heat.** Brown the sausage for 3–4 minutes. Place in a small bowl, cover, and refrigerate until needed.

3 **To pan residue, add 1/2 cup broth and scrape the bottom and sides to release any browned bits.** Place in the slow cooker with the remaining broth, tomatoes, potatoes, onion, corn, seafood seasoning, oregano, and thyme. Cover and cook on high for 2 1/2 hours, or on low for 5 hours, or until vegetables are tender.

4 **Add the sausage and remaining ingredients.** Cover and cook on high for 30 minutes.

CHILIS SOUPS CH

SOUPS

CHILI

SOUPS CHILIS SOUPS CHILIS SOUPS CHILIS SOUPS CHILIS SOUPS CHILIS SOUPS CHILIS SOUPS CHILIS SOUPS CHILIS SOUPS **SOUPS** CHILIS SOUPS CHILIS

Spicy Shrimp, Spicy Thai Soup

Makes 4 cups
Serves: 4
Serving Size: 1 cup

**Exchanges/
Food Choices:**
3 Vegetable
1 Lean Meat
1/2 Fat

Calories	150
Calories from Fat	35
Total Fat	4g
Saturated Fat	0g
Trans Fat	0g
Monounsaturated Fat	0g
Cholesterol	65mg
Sodium	400mg
Potassium	808mg
Total Carbohydrate	14g
Dietary Fiber	3g
Sugars	4g
Protein	15g

Nonstick cooking spray

4 ounces whole mushrooms, wiped with a damp cloth and quartered

2 cups (1 pint) grape tomatoes, halved

8 ounces frozen pepper stir-fry

1 1/2 cups water

1 tablespoon sodium-free chicken bouillon granules

1 teaspoon dried basil leaves

1 teaspoon ground ginger

1/2 teaspoon dried pepper flakes, or to taste

8 ounces raw shrimp, peeled

1/2 13-ounce can light coconut milk

1/2 cup chopped cilantro leaves

1/2 teaspoon salt

1 medium lime, quartered

1 **Coat a 3 1/2- to 4-quart slow cooker with cooking spray.** Place the mushrooms, tomatoes, pepper stir-fry, water, bouillon, basil, ginger, and pepper flakes in the slow cooker. Cover and cook on high for 3 1/2 hours, or on low for 7 hours, or until vegetables are tender.

2 **Stir in the shrimp, cover, and cook on high 20 minutes or until shrimp are opaque.** Stir in the remaining ingredients, except the lime. Serve with lime wedges to squeeze over all.

Cook's Note:
Be sure to shake the unopened can of coconut milk vigorously before opening. It has a tendency to separate after sitting for long periods.

Lentil-Ginger Soup

Makes 8 cups
Serves: 8
Serving Size: 1 cup soup,
2 tablespoons yogurt,
1 1/2 teaspoons cilantro, and
1 lime wedge

**Exchanges/
Food Choices:**
2 Starch
1 Vegetable
1 Lean Meat
1/2 Fat

Calories	240
Calories from Fat	40
Total Fat	4.5g
Saturated Fat	0g
Trans Fat	0g
Monounsaturated Fat	2g
Cholesterol	0mg
Sodium	410mg
Potassium	513mg
Total Carbohydrate	38g
Dietary Fiber	10g
Sugars	6g
Protein	14g

Nonstick cooking spray

2 tablespoons canola oil

1 cup diced onion

1/2 cup diced carrots

5 cups no-salt-added
vegetable broth

2 cups dried brown lentils

14.5-ounce can no-salt-
added stewed tomatoes

2 teaspoons curry powder

1 teaspoon ground cumin

1/2 teaspoon dried pepper
flakes

1 1/4 cups chopped fresh
cilantro leaves, divided

1–1 1/2 tablespoons
grated gingerroot

1 teaspoon salt

1 cup fat-free plain Greek
yogurt

1 medium lime, cut into
8 wedges

1. **Coat a 3 1/2- to 4-quart slow cooker with cooking spray.**

2. **Heat the oil in a large nonstick skillet over medium-high heat.** Cook the onion and carrots 4–5 minutes or until golden on edges, stirring occasionally.

3. **Place in the slow cooker with the broth, lentils, tomatoes, curry, cumin, and pepper flakes.** Cover and cook on high for 3 hours, or on low for 6 hours, or until vegetables are tender.

4. **Turn off the heat.** Stir in 1 cup cilantro, the ginger, and the salt and let stand, uncovered, 15 minutes to absorb flavors. Serve topped with yogurt, remaining cilantro, and lime wedges to squeeze over all.

Cook's Note:
Freezes well.

CHILIS SOUPS CHILIS CH

SOUPS

CHILIS SOUPS CHILIS SOUPS CHILIS SOUPS CHILIS SOUPS CHILIS SOUPS CHILIS SOUPS CHILIS SOUPS CHILIS **SOUPS** CHILIS SOUPS

Chunky Italian Garden Veggie Soup

Makes 9 cups
Serves: 6
Serving Size: 1 1/2 cups

Exchanges/ Food Choices:

1 Starch
3 Vegetable
1 Lean Meat
1 Fat

Calories	240
Calories from Fat	60
Total Fat	7g
Saturated Fat	2g
Trans Fat	0g
Monounsaturated Fat	3.5g
Cholesterol	10mg
Sodium	490mg
Potassium	839mg
Total Carbohydrate	33g
Dietary Fiber	11g
Sugars	11g
Protein	15g

Nonstick cooking spray

8 ounces whole mushrooms, wiped clean with a damp cloth and quartered

2 medium yellow squash, quartered lengthwise and cut into 1-inch pieces

2 medium green bell peppers, cut into 1-inch cubes

1 1/2 cups coarsely chopped onion

2 teaspoons dried oregano leaves

1/4 teaspoon dried pepper flakes

2 14.5-ounce cans no-salt-added stewed tomatoes

3 cups fresh baby spinach

15-ounce can no-salt-added navy beans, rinsed and drained

1/2 cup chopped fresh basil leaves

1 tablespoon extra-virgin olive oil

1/2 teaspoon salt

12 pitted kalamata olives, coarsely chopped

3/4 cup shredded part-skim mozzarella cheese

1 **Coat a 5- to 6-quart slow cooker with cooking spray.**

2 **Place the mushrooms, squash, bell peppers, onions, oregano, and pepper flakes in the slow cooker, top with the tomatoes.** Cover and cook for 4 hours on high, or for 7 1/2–8 hours on low, or until vegetables are tender.

3 **Stir in the spinach, beans, basil, oil, and salt.** Turn off the heat, cover and let stand 15 minutes to heat thoroughly.

4 **Spoon equal amounts in six shallow soup bowls, about 1 1/2 cups per bowl, and sprinkle evenly with the olives and cheese.** The heat from the soup will slightly melt the cheese.

Cook's Note:

Serve as is or over 3 cups cooked whole-grain rotini pasta, if desired.

Fresh Fennel Bean Soup with Parmesan

Makes 6 cups
Serves: 6
Serving Size: 1 cup

**Exchanges/
Food Choices:**
2 Starch
1 Vegetable
1 Lean Meat
1/2 Fat

Calories	250
Calories from Fat	50
Total Fat	5g
Saturated Fat	1.5g
Trans Fat	0g
Monounsaturated Fat	1g
Cholesterol	5mg
Sodium	640mg
Potassium	748mg
Total Carbohydrate	39g
Dietary Fiber	12g
Sugars	4g
Protein	11g

Nonstick cooking spray

2 tablespoons extra-virgin olive oil, divided

1 medium fennel bulb, thinly sliced

1 1/2 cups diced onion

1 cup sliced carrots

1 cup diced red potatoes

2 1/2 cups water

1 teaspoon dried thyme leaves

1/2 teaspoon garlic powder

1 dried bay leaf

2 15-ounce cans no-salt-added Great Northern or other white bean, rinsed and drained

1 teaspoon salt

1 cup fat-free half-and-half

1 teaspoon finely chopped fresh rosemary or to taste

1/4 cup plus 2 tablespoons grated Parmesan cheese

1 medium lemon, cut into 6 wedges

1. **Coat a 3 1/2- to 4-quart slow cooker with cooking spray.**

2. **Heat 1 tablespoon of the oil in a large nonstick skillet over medium-high heat.** Cook the fennel and onions for 6 minutes or until golden on edges, stirring occasionally.

3. **Place in the slow cooker with the carrots, potatoes, water, thyme, garlic powder, and bay leaf.** Cover and cook on high for 3 1/2 hours, or on low for 7 hours, or until vegetables are tender.

4. **Turn off heat.** Stir in the remaining ingredients, except the cheese and lemon wedges. Let stand 30 minutes to absorb flavors. Sprinkle cheese on top of each serving and serve lemon wedges to squeeze over all.

Gingered Pumpkin Bisque

Makes 6 cups
Serves: 6
Serving Size: 1 cup soup
and 1 tablespoon yogurt

**Exchanges/
Food Choices:**
1 1/2 Carbohydrate
1 Fat

Calories	170
Calories from Fat	35
Total Fat	4g
Saturated Fat	1g
Trans Fat	0g
Monounsaturated Fat	1.5g
Cholesterol	0mg
Sodium	400mg
Potassium	408mg
Total Carbohydrate	23g
Dietary Fiber	4g
Sugars	8g
Protein	3g

Nonstick cooking spray

15-ounce can pumpkin

1 firm medium pear,
peeled, cored, and
chopped

1 1/2 cups diced onion

14.5-ounce can reduced-
sodium chicken broth

1/2 teaspoon ground
cumin

1/4 teaspoon ground
nutmeg

1/4 teaspoon salt

1/8 teaspoon cayenne
pepper

2 cups fat-free half-and-
half

1/4 cup trans-fat-free
margarine

1 1/2 tablespoons packed
brown sugar substitute
blend, such as Splenda

2–3 teaspoons grated
gingerroot

1/4 cup plus 2 tablespoons
fat-free plain Greek
yogurt

1 **Coat a 3 1/2- to 4-quart slow
cooker with cooking spray.** Place
the pumpkin, pears, onions, broth,
cumin, nutmeg, salt, and cayenne in
the slow cooker. Cover and cook on
high for 3 1/2 hours, or on low for
7 hours, or until onions are tender.

2 **Working in 1-cup batches, purée
the pumpkin mixture in a blender,
being sure to secure the lid tightly
while puréeing.** Return the mixture
to the slow cooker, stir in the
remaining ingredients, except the
yogurt. Cover and cook on high for
30 minutes.

3 **Serve topped with equal amounts
of yogurt.**

Stews and Ragouts

Saucy Green Pepper Chicken

Makes 8 chicken pieces and 1 1/3 cups sauce
Serves: 4
Serving Size: 1 drumstick, 1 thigh, and 1/3 cup sauce

Exchanges/ Food Choices:
1 Vegetable
4 Lean Meat
1/2 Fat

Calories	220
Calories from Fat	70
Total Fat	8g
Saturated Fat	2g
Trans Fat	0g
Monounsaturated Fat	2.5g
Cholesterol	95mg
Sodium	550mg
Potassium	401mg
Total Carbohydrate	8g
Dietary Fiber	2g
Sugars	6g
Protein	27g

Nonstick cooking spray

1 large green bell pepper, cut into 1/2-inch strips

1 medium onion (4 ounces), cut into 8 wedges

4 chicken drumsticks, skin removed

4 bone-in chicken thighs, skin removed and trimmed of fat

2 tablespoons no-salt-added tomato paste

1 1/2 tablespoons cider vinegar

2 teaspoons sugar

1 teaspoon paprika

1 teaspoon dried oregano leaves

3/4 teaspoon salt

1/2 teaspoon black pepper

1 teaspoon Worcestershire sauce

1 **Coat a 3 1/2- to 4-quart slow cooker with cooking spray.** Place the bell pepper and onions in the slow cooker. Arrange the chicken pieces on top.

2 **In a small bowl, stir together the remaining ingredients.** Pour over all. Cover and cook on high for 3 1/2 hours, or on low for 7 hours, or until chicken is done.

Cook's Note:
May serve over choice of pasta, rice, or potatoes.

Whole Garlic Chicken Drums

Makes 8 drumsticks and 2 cups sauce
Serves: 4
Serving Size: 2 drumsticks and 1/2 cup sauce

**Exchanges/
Food Choices:**
2 Vegetable
3 Lean Meat

Calories	200
Calories from Fat	40
Total Fat	4.5g
Saturated Fat	1g
Trans Fat	0g
Monounsaturated Fat	1g
Cholesterol	95mg
Sodium	550mg
Potassium	399mg
Total Carbohydrate	11g
Dietary Fiber	1g
Sugars	2g
Protein	27g

Nonstick cooking spray

1 large onion (6 ounces), thinly sliced

20 medium garlic cloves, peeled

1/4 cup plus 2 tablespoons water, divided

1 teaspoon paprika

1 teaspoon dried oregano leaves

1/4 teaspoon dried rosemary

1/2 teaspoon black pepper

8 chicken drumsticks, skin removed

1 tablespoon cornstarch

3/4 teaspoon salt

1 **Coat a 3 1/2- to 4-quart slow cooker with cooking spray.** Place the onion, garlic, and 1/4 cup water in the slow cooker.

2 **In a small bowl, combine the paprika, oregano, rosemary, and black pepper.** Sprinkle evenly over the chicken pieces.

3 **Arrange the chicken over the onions, overlapping slightly.** Cover and cook on high for 3 1/2 hours, or on low for 7 hours, or until chicken is tender. Remove chicken and cover to keep warm.

4 **In a small bowl, stir together the remaining 2 tablespoons water and the cornstarch until cornstarch is dissolved.** Stir into the onion mixture with the salt, stirring briskly to break up large pieces of garlic and onion. Cover and cook on high 15 minutes to thicken. Spoon over the chicken.

Cook's Note:
Serve over your choice of pasta, rice, or potatoes.

STEWS RAGOUTS STEWS RAGOUTS S
STEWS
RAGOUTS STEWS
RAGOUTS STEWS
RAGOUTS STEWS
RAGOUTS STEWS
STEWS RAGOUTS
STEWS RAGOUTS

Sweet-Hot Drums

Makes 8 drumsticks and 2 cups sauce

Serves: 4
Serving Size: 2 drumsticks and 1/2 cup sauce

**Exchanges/
Food Choices:**
2 1/2 Carbohydrate
3 Lean Meat

Calories	320
Calories from Fat	40
Total Fat	4.5g
Saturated Fat	1g
Trans Fat	0g
Monounsaturated Fat	1g
Cholesterol	95mg
Sodium	500mg
Potassium	427mg
Total Carbohydrate	35g
Dietary Fiber	1g
Sugars	31g
Protein	27g

Nonstick cooking spray

8 chicken drumsticks, skin removed

2/3 cup apricot fruit spread

3 tablespoons light soy sauce

3 tablespoons no-salt-added tomato paste

1 1/2 tablespoons packed brown sugar substitute blend, such as Splenda

2 1/2 tablespoons balsamic vinegar

3 medium garlic cloves, minced

1/2 teaspoon dried pepper flakes

2 tablespoons water

1 tablespoon cornstarch

1 **Coat a 3 1/2- to 4-quart slow cooker with cooking spray.** Place the drumsticks in the slow cooker.

2 **In a medium bowl, stir together the remaining ingredients, except the water and cornstarch.** Pour over the chicken. Cover and cook on high for 3 hours, or on low for 6 hours, or until chicken is done.

3 **Remove the chicken and place on serving platter.** Cover to keep warm.

4 **In a small bowl, combine the water and cornstarch.** Stir until cornstarch is completely dissolved. Stir into the slow cooker. Cover and cook on high 15 minutes to thicken. Pour sauce over the chicken.

Cook's Note:
Serve over your choice of pasta, rice, or potatoes.

Rough-Cut Chicken with Dried Onions and Mushrooms

Makes 4 chicken breast pieces and 2 cups mushroom mixture
Serves: 4
Serving Size: 3 ounces cooked chicken and 1/2 cup mushroom mixture

Exchanges/ Food Choices:
1 Carbohydrate
5 Lean Meat

Calories	220
Calories from Fat	80
Total Fat	9g
Saturated Fat	1.5g
Trans Fat	0g
Monounsaturated Fat	5.5g
Cholesterol	45mg
Sodium	370mg
Potassium	630mg
Total Carbohydrate	15g
Dietary Fiber	2g
Sugars	5g
Protein	20g

Nonstick cooking spray

8 ounces sliced mushrooms

1 1/2 cups diced onion

2 12-ounce skinless chicken breasts with bone in, cut in half through the bone

1/2 teaspoon dried thyme leaves

1-ounce packet dried onion soup mix

2 tablespoons extra-virgin olive oil

1 tablespoon cornstarch

2 tablespoons water

1 **Coat a 3 1/2- to 4-quart slow cooker with cooking spray.** Place the mushrooms and onions in the slow cooker.

2 **Place the chicken pieces on top and sprinkle evenly with the thyme and soup mix; drizzle oil over all.** Cover and cook on high for 2 1/2–3 hours, or on low for 5–6 hours, or until chicken is no longer pink in center.

3 **Remove chicken with a slotted spoon and place on separate plate.**

4 **In a small bowl, stir together the cornstarch and water until cornstarch is completely dissolved, and stir into the slow cooker.** Cover and cook on high setting 15 minutes or until thickened. Spoon over the chicken pieces.

Cook's Note:
For a thicker mushroom mixture, use 1 tablespoon plus 1 teaspoon cornstarch.

Smoky Red Chicken

Makes 4 chicken breasts and 2 cups sauce

Serves: 4
Serving Size: 3 ounces cooked chicken and 1/2 cup sauce

Exchanges/ Food Choices:
2 Vegetable
2 Lean Meat
1/2 Fat

Calories	170
Calories from Fat	50
Total Fat	6g
Saturated Fat	1g
Trans Fat	0g
Monounsaturated Fat	3g
Cholesterol	45mg
Sodium	410mg
Potassium	141mg
Total Carbohydrate	9g
Dietary Fiber	1g
Sugars	3g
Protein	18g

Nonstick cooking spray

4 4-ounce boneless, skinless chicken breasts, trimmed of fat

1-ounce packet 40%-less-sodium taco seasoning

1/2 teaspoon smoked paprika or chipotle powder

14.5-ounce can no-salt-added diced tomatoes, drained

1 tablespoon extra-virgin olive oil

1/4 cup chopped fresh cilantro leaves

1 **Coat a 3 1/2- to 4-quart slow cooker with cooking spray.** Place the chicken in the slow cooker.

2 **Sprinkle the taco seasoning and paprika evenly over the chicken and pour the tomatoes over all.** Cover and cook on high for 1 hour and 45 minutes, or on low for 3 1/2 hours, or until chicken is no longer pink in center.

3 **Place chicken pieces on a serving plate.** Stir the oil and cilantro into the tomato mixture in the slow cooker and spoon over the chicken.

Asian Bundle Lettuce Wraps, page 37

Mediterranean Eggplant Mounds, page 132

Sweet-Hot Drums, page 70

Coconut Vegetable Curry, page 93

Pico de Gallo Cod with Avocado, page 128

Pulled Pork with Tomato-Green Chili Chipotle Sauce, page 86

Wheat Berries, Edamame, and Black Bean Toss, page 135

Meatloaf on a Sling, page 113

Burgundy Beef and Mushrooms, page 80

Gingered Pumpkin Bisque, page 66

Chicken Pot Biscuits, page 102

Family Table Tamale Pie, page 115

One-Pot Comfort Shepherd's Pie, page 114

Buttery Black Pepper-Parsley Cob Corn, page 146
Chop-Free Chili, page 57

Slow Salmon with Horseradish-Dill Sour Cream, page 129

Individual Peach-Pineapple Crumblers, page 170

Chicken Breasts with Sun-Dried Tomato Sauce

Makes 4 chicken breasts and 2 cups sauce
Serves: 4
Serving Size: 3 ounces cooked chicken and 1/2 cup sauce

**Exchanges/
Food Choices:**
1/2 Starch
1 Vegetable
2 Lean Meat
1 Fat

Calories	190
Calories from Fat	60
Total Fat	7g
Saturated Fat	1.5g
Trans Fat	0g
Monounsaturated Fat	3.5g
Cholesterol	50mg
Sodium	130mg
Potassium	500mg
Total Carbohydrate	12g
Dietary Fiber	2g
Sugars	7g
Protein	19g

Nonstick cooking spray

1 medium zucchini, thinly sliced

1/4 cup diced onion

8 sun-dried tomato halves, cut in thin strips

4 4-ounce boneless, skinless chicken breasts, trimmed of fat

1 tablespoon dried basil leaves

1 cup prepared spaghetti sauce

1 tablespoon extra-virgin olive oil

1 **Coat a 3 1/2- to 4-quart slow cooker with cooking spray.** Place the zucchini, onion, and sun-dried tomato strips in the slow cooker.

2 **Arrange the chicken pieces on top, overlapping slightly.** Sprinkle evenly with the basil. Cover and cook on high for 1 1/2 hours or on low for 3 hours.

3 **In a small bowl, stir together the spaghetti sauce and the oil.** Spoon the sauce over the chicken. Cover and cook on high for 15 minutes.

Cook's Note:
Omit the oil and sprinkle with 1/2 cup crumbled feta cheese for added flavor.

Cheese-Topped Creamy Chicken

Makes 3 cups
Serves: 4
Serving Size: 3/4 cup

**Exchanges/
Food Choices:**
1 Carbohydrate
3 Lean Meat

Calories	190
Calories from Fat	40
Total Fat	4.5g
Saturated Fat	2g
Trans Fat	0g
Monounsaturated Fat	0.5g
Cholesterol	55mg
Sodium	500mg
Potassium	414mg
Total Carbohydrate	13g
Dietary Fiber	2g
Sugars	4g
Protein	21g

Nonstick cooking spray

3 ounces sliced mushrooms

1 cup diced onion

1 cup diced red bell pepper

1–2 medium garlic cloves, minced

1/2 cup dry white wine or reduced-sodium chicken broth, divided

12 ounces boneless, skinless chicken breast halves

1/4 teaspoon dried thyme leaves

1/4 teaspoon black pepper

2 tablespoons cornstarch

1/3 cup fat-free half-and-half

1/2 teaspoon salt

1/3 cup grated Parmesan cheese or shredded reduced-fat sharp Cheddar cheese

1 **Coat a 3 1/2- to 4-quart slow cooker with cooking spray.** Stir together the mushrooms, onion, bell pepper, garlic, and 1/4 cup wine in the slow cooker.

2 **Top with the chicken pieces and sprinkle the thyme and black pepper evenly over all.** Cover and cook on high for 2 1/2 hours, or on low for 4 1/2–5 hours, or until chicken is no longer pink in center.

3 **Remove chicken pieces and place on cutting board.** In a small bowl, stir together the remaining 1/4 cup wine and the cornstarch. Stir into the mushroom mixture. Cover and cook on high for 15 minutes or until sauce thickens.

4 **Roughly shred chicken and return to the slow cooker with the half-and-half and the salt.** Sprinkle with cheese.

Creamy Chicken and Rough-Cut Veggie Stew

Makes 8 cups
Serves: 8
Serving Size: 1 cup soup plus 1 tablespoon cheese

**Exchanges/
Food Choices:**
1 Starch
1 Vegetable
3 Lean Meat

Calories	240
Calories from Fat	60
Total Fat	7g
Saturated Fat	2g
Trans Fat	0g
Monounsaturated Fat	1.5g
Cholesterol	60mg
Sodium	420mg
Potassium	924mg
Total Carbohydrate	20g
Dietary Fiber	2g
Sugars	6g
Protein	24g

Nonstick cooking spray

8 ounces carrots, peeled, quartered lengthwise, and cut into 2-inch pieces

1 pound red potatoes, cut into 1-inch cubes

1 cup diced yellow onion

4 medium garlic cloves, minced

2 teaspoons sodium-free chicken bouillon granules

1/2 cup water

1 1/2 pounds bone-in chicken breasts, skinned

1 teaspoon dried thyme leaves

1/4 teaspoon poultry seasoning or dried sage

1 cup fat-free sour cream

3/4 cup finely chopped green onions, divided

1 tablespoon extra-virgin olive oil

1/2 teaspoon salt

1/2 cup grated Parmesan cheese

1 **Coat a 3 1/2- to 4-quart slow cooker with cooking spray.** Stir together the carrots, potatoes, yellow onions, garlic, bouillon granules, and water in the slow cooker.

2 **Place the chicken breasts on top of the vegetables.** Sprinkle evenly with the thyme and poultry seasoning. Cover and cook on high for 3 hours, or on low for 6 hours, or until chicken is no longer pink in center.

3 **Turn off the heat.** Remove the chicken and place on separate plate. Gently stir the sour cream, 1/2 cup green onions, oil, and salt into the remaining ingredients in the slow cooker. Cover and let stand 15 minutes to absorb flavors.

4 **Meanwhile, debone and roughly shred the chicken.** Gently stir the chicken into the potato mixture. Serve in bowls and sprinkle evenly with the remaining green onions and the Parmesan cheese.

Kalamata-Basil Chicken

Makes 5 cups
Serves: 4
Serving Size: 1 1/4 cups

**Exchanges/
Food Choices:**
3 Vegetable
3 Lean Meat
1 Fat

Calories	260
Calories from Fat	80
Total Fat	8g
Saturated Fat	2.5g
Trans Fat	0g
Monounsaturated Fat	3.5g
Cholesterol	80mg
Sodium	550mg
Potassium	926mg
Total Carbohydrate	15g
Dietary Fiber	3g
Sugars	9g
Protein	30g

Nonstick cooking spray

1 medium zucchini, cut into 1/2-inch slices

1 medium green bell pepper, cut into thin strips

1 medium onion (4 ounces), cut into 1/2-inch wedges

4 ounces sliced mushrooms

4 4-ounce boneless, skinless chicken breasts, trimmed of fat

1/2 6-ounce can no-salt-added tomato paste

1/3 cup balsamic vinegar

1/2 teaspoon garlic powder

1/4 teaspoon dried pepper flakes

1/4 cup chopped fresh basil leaves

10 pitted kalamata olives, coarsely chopped

1/4 teaspoon salt

2 ounces (1/2 cup) part-skim mozzarella cheese, shredded

1   **Coat a 6-quart slow cooker with cooking spray.** Place the zucchini, peppers, onions, and mushrooms in the slow cooker and place the chicken on top in a single layer.

2   **In a small bowl, combine tomato paste, vinegar, garlic powder, and pepper flakes.** Pour over all, cover, and cook on high for 3–3 1/2 hours, or on low for 6–7 hours, or until the onions are tender.

3   **Remove chicken pieces and place on cutting board.** Roughly shred chicken and return to the slow cooker with the basil, olives, and salt. Stir gently and sprinkle the cheese over all. Turn off the heat, cover, and let stand 5 minutes to allow cheese to melt.

Chicken-Apple Sausage and Cabbage

Makes 3 cups cabbage mixture and 4 halved sausage links
Serves: 4
Serving Size: 3/4 cup cabbage mixture and 1 halved sausage link

Exchanges/ Food Choices:
1/2 Starch
2 Vegetable
1 Lean Meat
1 Fat

Calories	180
Calories from Fat	60
Total Fat	7g
Saturated Fat	2g
Trans Fat	0g
Monounsaturated Fat	0.5g
Cholesterol	50mg
Sodium	590mg
Potassium	338mg
Total Carbohydrate	20g
Dietary Fiber	6g
Sugars	8g
Protein	11g

Nonstick cooking spray

8 ounces green cabbage, coarsely chopped into 1-inch pieces

1 large green bell pepper, cut into 1-inch chunks

1 medium onion (4 ounces), cut into 8 wedges

1 teaspoon canola oil

2 3-ounce chicken and apple sausage links, split in half lengthwise

1/2 cup water

2 tablespoons ketchup

1/4 teaspoon dried fennel seed, *optional*

1/2 15-ounce can no-salt-added navy or other white bean, rinsed and drained

1/4 teaspoon salt

1 **Coat a 3 1/2- to 4-quart slow cooker with cooking spray.** Place the cabbage, bell peppers, and onions in the slow cooker.

2 **Heat the oil in a medium nonstick skillet over medium heat.** Brown the sausage 2 minutes on each side. Remove the skillet from the heat. Place the sausage on a separate plate, cover, and refrigerate until needed.

3 **Add the water, ketchup, and the fennel to the skillet and scrape the bottom and sides to release any browned bits.** Pour over the cabbage mixture. Cover and cook on high for 2 1/2 hours, or on low for 5 hours, or until vegetables are tender.

4 **Turn off the heat.** Stir in beans and salt. Place the sausage on top, cut side down, cover, and let stand 15 minutes to heat and absorb flavors.

Cook's Note:
Serve over your choice of pasta, rice, or potatoes.

Hearty, Homey Sausage and Lentils

Makes 6 cups
Serves: 6
Serving Size: 1 cup

**Exchanges/
Food Choices:**
1 1/2 Starch
1 Medium-Fat Meat
1 Fat

Calories	230
Calories from Fat	80
Total Fat	9g
Saturated Fat	1.5g
Trans Fat	0g
Monounsaturated Fat	4.5g
Cholesterol	25mg
Sodium	460mg
Potassium	757mg
Total Carbohydrate	25g
Dietary Fiber	6g
Sugars	4g
Protein	13g

Nonstick cooking spray

1 cup dried lentils, sorted for stones and shriveled lentils and rinsed

1 cup diced onion

3 1/4 cups water, divided

1 tablespoon sodium-free chicken bouillon granules

1 cup diced green bell pepper

1 dried bay leaf

1 teaspoon dried oregano leaves

1/4 teaspoon dried red pepper flakes

8 ounces smoked turkey sausage, diced

1/2 cup chopped fresh parsley

2 tablespoons extra-virgin olive oil

1/4 teaspoon salt

1 **Coat a 3 1/2- to 4-quart slow cooker with cooking spray.**

2 **Stir in the lentils, onions, 3 cups water, bouillon, bell pepper, bay leaf, oregano, and pepper flakes.** Cover and cook on high for 2 hours, or on low for 3 1/2–4 hours, or until lentils are tender.

3 **Thirty minutes before serving, heat a medium skillet coated with cooking spray over medium-high heat.** Brown the sausage. Stir into the lentils with the parsley, oil, and salt. Add the remaining 1/4 cup water to the pan residue in the skillet, scraping the bottom and sides, and add to the lentil mixture.

4 **Cover the slow cooker, turn off the heat, and let stand 15 minutes to absorb flavors.** Serve in bowls, if desired.

Creamy Beef with Dilled Mushrooms

Makes 3 cups
Serves: 4
Serving Size: 3/4 cup

**Exchanges/
Food Choices:**
2 Vegetable
3 Lean Meat
1/2 Fat

Calories	210
Calories from Fat	60
Total Fat	7g
Saturated Fat	2.5g
Trans Fat	0g
Monounsaturated Fat	1.5g
Cholesterol	80mg
Sodium	570mg
Potassium	502mg
Total Carbohydrate	9g
Dietary Fiber	1g
Sugars	4g
Protein	27g

Nonstick cooking spray

1 pound trimmed extra-lean chuck roast, cut into bite-size pieces

4 medium garlic cloves, minced

1 cup water, divided

8 ounces sliced mushrooms

1 cup diced onion

1 tablespoon steak sauce, such as A-1

4 wedges light herb and garlic cream cheese spread, such as Laughing Cow, cut into small pieces

2 teaspoons Dijon mustard

1/2 teaspoon dried dill weed

1/2 teaspoon black pepper

1/4 teaspoon salt

1 **Coat a 3 1/2- to 4-quart slow cooker with cooking spray.**

2 **Heat a large skillet coated with cooking spray over medium-high heat.** Brown the beef about 3–4 minutes, adding the garlic for the last 15 seconds, stirring occasionally. Place the beef in the slow cooker.

3 **Add 1/4 cup water to the skillet and scrape the bottom and sides to release any browned bits.** Pour into the slow cooker with the mushrooms, onions, and steak sauce. Stir until well blended. Cover and cook on high only for 4 hours or until beef is tender.

4 **Turn off the heat.** Remove lid, stir in the remaining ingredients. Cover and let stand 15 minutes to absorb flavors.

Burgundy Beef and Mushrooms

Makes 6 cups
Serves: 8
Serving Size: 3/4 cup

**Exchanges/
Food Choices:**
3 Vegetables
3 Lean Meat
1/2 Fat

Calories	230
Calories from Fat	45
Total Fat	5g
Saturated Fat	2g
Trans Fat	0g
Monounsaturated Fat	2g
Cholesterol	75mg
Sodium	340mg
Potassium	864mg
Total Carbohydrate	13g
Dietary Fiber	2g
Sugars	6g
Protein	26g

Nonstick cooking spray

2 pounds trimmed, boneless, extra-lean chuck roast, cut into 2-inch pieces

1 1/2 cups dry red wine, divided

2 cups sliced carrots

1 1/2 cups diced onion

4 ounces sliced mushrooms

8 whole garlic cloves, peeled

14.5-ounce can no-salt-added diced tomatoes

2 tablespoons no-salt-added tomato paste

2 teaspoons sodium-free beef bouillon granules

2 teaspoons sugar

1/2 teaspoon dried rosemary

1/2 teaspoon dried oregano leaves

1 dried bay leaf

1/8 teaspoon ground allspice

3/4 teaspoon salt

1 **Coat a 3 1/2- to 4-quart slow cooker with cooking spray.**

2 **Heat a large skillet coated with cooking spray over medium-high heat.** Working in two batches, brown the beef 3–4 minutes, stirring occasionally. Place the beef in the slow cooker.

3 **To the pan residue, add 1/2 cup wine and scrape the bottom and sides to release any browned bits.** Pour in the slow cooker with the remaining ingredients, except the salt. Cover and cook on high for 5 hours, or on low for 9–10 hours, or until beef is very tender.

4 **Turn off the heat, stir in the salt, and let stand, uncovered, 15 minutes to absorb flavors.**

Cook's Note:

When purchasing chuck, even the extra-lean variety, be sure to purchase 6–8 ounces more than needed, because there will be fat underneath the piece that needs to be trimmed out before cooking.

Family-Style Chuck and Veggies

Makes 12 cups
Serves: 8
Serving Size: 1 1/2 cups

**Exchanges/
Food Choices:**
1 Starch
3 Vegetable
3 Lean Meat

Calories	270
Calories from Fat	40
Total Fat	4.5g
Saturated Fat	1.5g
Trans Fat	0g
Monounsaturated Fat	1.5g
Cholesterol	70mg
Sodium	520mg
Potassium	915mg
Total Carbohydrate	31g
Dietary Fiber	4g
Sugars	10g
Protein	26g

LIGHTLY SALT & PEPPER MEAT

Nonstick cooking spray
LESS 1 1/2 pounds new potatoes, halved
LESS 1 pound baby carrots
2 medium onions (8 ounces total), cut into 1/2-inch wedges
LESS 2 medium green bell peppers, cut into 1/2-inch-wide strips *FROZEN SLICED*
2 medium celery stalks, cut into 2-inch pieces
1/2 cup water *BROTH*
2 pounds trimmed, extra-lean, boneless chuck roast
1/3 cup ketchup, divided
1 tablespoon Worcestershire sauce
2 teaspoons dried oregano leaves
2 teaspoons garlic powder
1/2 teaspoon ground allspice
1 tablespoon sodium-free beef bouillon granules
1 teaspoon black pepper
1 teaspoon salt

1 **Coat a 6-quart slow cooker with cooking spray.** Place the potatoes, carrots, onions, peppers, celery, and water in the slow cooker. Top with the beef.

2 **In a small bowl, combine 1 tablespoon ketchup, the Worcestershire sauce, oregano, garlic powder, and allspice.** Spread evenly over the beef and sprinkle with the bouillon granules and black pepper. Cover and cook on high for 5 hours or on low for 9 1/2–10 hours, or until beef is very tender. *3 1/2 HRS HIGH*

3 **Using two forks, gently pull the beef apart in 2-inch chunks, if possible, in the slow cooker.** Gently stir in the remaining ketchup and salt. Cover and cook on high for 15 minutes to absorb flavors.

Cook's Note:

When purchasing chuck roasts, buy approximately 6–8 ounces more than the recipe indicates, because often there will be 6–8 ounces of fat that has to be trimmed, even on roasts that are labeled "lean." Also, for a thicker consistency, mix 2 teaspoons cornstarch with the remaining ketchup and salt, then add to the beef mixture.

Smoky Bacon Beef Goulash

Makes 8 cups
Serves: 8
Serving Size: 1 cup

**Exchanges/
Food Choices:**
2 Vegetable
6 Lean Meat

Calories	320
Calories from Fat	90
Total Fat	10g
Saturated Fat	3.5g
Trans Fat	0g
Monounsaturated Fat	3g
Cholesterol	125mg
Sodium	560mg
Potassium	756mg
Total Carbohydrate	10g
Dietary Fiber	2g
Sugars	5g
Protein	45g

Nonstick cooking spray

2 pounds trimmed, extra-lean, boneless chuck roast, cut into 1-inch pieces

1 1/2 tablespoons smoked paprika

1 tablespoon sodium-free beef bouillon granules

1 teaspoon garlic powder

1/2 teaspoon dried oregano leaves

1/2 teaspoon black pepper

1 1/2 cups diced onion

1 cup diced red bell pepper

4 ounces sliced mushrooms

14.5-ounce can no-salt-added stewed tomatoes

1/2 cup water

1 teaspoon Worcestershire sauce

3-ounce package natural bacon bits

1/2 teaspoon salt

1 **Coat a 3 1/2- to 4-quart slow cooker with cooking spray.** Place beef in the slow cooker. Sprinkle evenly with the paprika, bouillon granules, garlic powder, oregano, and black pepper. Toss until well coated.

2 **Top with the remaining ingredients, except the bacon and salt.** Cover and cook on high for 4 1/2 hours, or on low for 8–9 hours, or until beef is very tender.

3 **Turn off the heat, remove lid, stir in the bacon, and let stand, uncovered, for 30 minutes to absorb flavors.** Stir in the salt.

Slow Go Chuck with Molasses

Makes about 7 cups
Serves: 6
Serving Size: 1 1/4 cups

**Exchanges/
Food Choices:**
1 Carbohydrate
2 Vegetable
3 Lean Meat

Calories	260
Calories from Fat	50
Total Fat	6g
Saturated Fat	2g
Trans Fat	0g
Monounsaturated Fat	2.5g
Cholesterol	80mg
Sodium	500mg
Potassium	824mg
Total Carbohydrate	23g
Dietary Fiber	4g
Sugars	15g
Protein	28g

Nonstick cooking spray

1 teaspoon canola oil

1 3/4 pounds trimmed, extra-lean, boneless chuck roast

1 1/2 cups water, divided

1 pound whole carrots, peeled, halved lengthwise, and cut into 3-inch pieces

2 medium onions (8 ounces total), quartered

1/4 cup molasses

3 tablespoons cider vinegar

3 tablespoons no-salt-added tomato paste

1 tablespoon instant coffee granules

1 tablespoon no-salt-added steak grilling seasoning blend

1/2–1 teaspoon ground cinnamon

1 teaspoon salt

1. **Coat a 6-quart slow cooker with cooking spray.**

2. **Heat the oil in a large nonstick skillet over medium-high heat.** Brown beef 3 minutes on each side. Place beef in slow cooker.

3. **Add 1/2 cup water to the skillet and scrape the bottom and sides to release any browned bits.** Pour over the beef. Place the carrots and onions in the slow cooker.

4. **In a medium bowl, whisk together the remaining ingredients.** Pour over all. Cover and cook on low only for 7 hours or until beef is tender and falling apart. Roughly pull apart the beef.

5. **Turn off the heat and let stand, uncovered, for 30 minutes to absorb flavors and thicken slightly.**

Cook's Note:
The flavors are even better the next day. So make it one day, chill, and serve it up the next night!

Sweet-Spiced Beef and Eggplant

Makes 4 cups
Serves: 4
Serving Size: 1 cup beef mixture and 2 tablespoons yogurt

**Exchanges/
Food Choices:**
1 Fruit
2 Vegetable
3 Lean Meat
1 1/2 Fat

Calories	310
Calories from Fat	110
Total Fat	13g
Saturated Fat	3g
Trans Fat	0g
Monounsaturated Fat	4g
Cholesterol	45mg
Sodium	390mg
Potassium	236mg
Total Carbohydrate	26g
Dietary Fiber	5g
Sugars	17g
Protein	23g

Nonstick cooking spray

8 ounces frozen pepper stir-fry, thawed

8 ounces chopped eggplant

1/3 cup raisins

8-ounce can no-salt-added tomato sauce

1/4 cup water

1/2 teaspoon dried thyme leaves

1 teaspoon apple pie spice **or** 3/4 teaspoon ground cinnamon and 1/4 teaspoon ground nutmeg

1/4 teaspoon dried pepper flakes

12 ounces extra-lean ground beef

2 ounces (1/2 cup) pine nuts, toasted

1 1/2 teaspoons sugar

1/2 teaspoon salt

1/2 cup fat-free plain Greek yogurt, *optional*

1 **Coat a 3 1/2- to 4-quart slow cooker with cooking spray.** Place pepper stir-fry, eggplant, raisins, tomato sauce, water, thyme, pie spice, and pepper flakes in the bottom of the slow cooker.

2 **Heat a large skillet coated with cooking spray over medium-high heat.** Brown the beef, stirring occasionally. Stir the beef into the ingredients in the slow cooker. Cover and cook on high for 3 hours, or on low for 6 hours, or until the vegetables are tender.

3 **Turn off the heat.** Stir the pine nuts, sugar, and salt into the beef mixture in the slow cooker and let stand, covered, 15 minutes to absorb flavors. Serve the beef mixture topped with the yogurt, if desired.

Stick-to-Your-Ribs Beef-Veggie Bowls

Makes 8 cups
Serves: 6
Serving Size: 1 1/3 cups

**Exchanges/
Food Choices:**
1/2 Starch
4 Vegetable
2 Lean Meat

Calories	230
Calories from Fat	35
Total Fat	4g
Saturated Fat	1.5g
Trans Fat	0g
Monounsaturated Fat	1g
Cholesterol	40mg
Sodium	510mg
Potassium	770 mg
Total Carbohydrate	30g
Dietary Fiber	7g
Sugars	13g
Protein	20g

Nonstick cooking spray

1 pound extra-lean
ground beef

16 ounces frozen pepper
stir-fry, thawed

2 cups frozen cut green
beans, thawed

14.5-ounce can no-salt-
added stewed tomatoes

1 1/2 cups water

1/3 cup ketchup

1/2 6-ounce can no-salt-
added tomato paste

1 tablespoon sodium-free
beef bouillon granules

1 tablespoon dried
oregano leaves

2 teaspoons
Worcestershire sauce

4 cups coarsely chopped
green cabbage

2 ounces uncooked
whole-grain macaroni
or rotini noodles

1/2 teaspoon salt

1. **Coat a 6-quart slow cooker with
cooking spray.**

2. **Heat a large skillet coated with
cooking spray over medium-high
heat.** Brown the beef 3–4 minutes,
stirring frequently.

3. **Place the beef in the slow cooker
with the pepper stir-fry, beans,
tomatoes, water, ketchup, tomato
paste, bouillon granules, oregano,
and Worcestershire sauce.** Stir until
well blended. Cover and cook on
high for 3 1/2 hours or on low for
7 hours.

4. **Stir in the cabbage and noodles.**
Cover and cook on high for
30 minutes until cabbage is
tender. Stir in the salt.

Cook's Note:
Be sure to coarsely chop the
cabbage (about 3/4–1 inch) for peak
texture and flavor.

Pulled Pork with Tomato-Green Chili Chipotle Sauce

Makes 4 cups shredded pork and 2 cups sauce
Serves: 8
Serving Size: 1/2 cup shredded pork and 1/4 cup sauce

Exchanges/ Food Choices:
1 Vegetable
2 Lean Meat
1/2 Fat

Calories	180
Calories from Fat	80
Total Fat	9g
Saturated Fat	2g
Trans Fat	0g
Monounsaturated Fat	4g
Cholesterol	45mg
Sodium	300mg
Potassium	526mg
Total Carbohydrate	8g
Dietary Fiber	2g
Sugars	4g
Protein	15g

Nonstick cooking spray

2 tablespoons extra-virgin olive oil

1 1/2 pounds boneless pork chops, trimmed of fat, divided

1/4 cup water

2 tablespoons chili powder

2 tablespoons minced dried onion

1 tablespoon sodium-free beef bouillon granules

2 teaspoons ground cumin

1/2 teaspoon garlic powder

1 medium chipotle chili pepper (canned in adobo sauce), minced

1 tablespoon adobo sauce

4-ounce can chopped mild green chilies

14.5-ounce can no-salt-added stewed tomatoes

1/2 teaspoon salt

1 **Coat a 6-quart slow cooker with cooking spray.**

2 **Heat 1 tablespoon oil in a large nonstick skillet over medium-high heat.** Working in two batches, brown the pork on one side only for 3–4 minutes. Place the pork, browned side up, in the slow cooker.

3 **Add the water to the skillet and scrape the bottom and sides to release any browned bits.** Pour into the slow cooker with the remaining ingredients, except the remaining 1 tablespoon oil and the salt. Cover and cook on high for 3 1/2 hours, or on low for 7 hours, or until pork is very tender.

4 **Remove the pork with a slotted spoon and shred.** Stir the remaining oil and salt into the ingredients in the slow cooker, breaking up large pieces of tomato.

Cumin Pork Stew with Corn

Makes 6 cups
Serves: 6
Serving Size: 1 cup

**Exchanges/
Food Choices:**
1/2 Starch
2 Vegetables
2 Lean Meat
1 1/2 Fat

Calories	240
Calories from Fat	90
Total Fat	10g
Saturated Fat	2g
Trans Fat	0g
Monounsaturated Fat	3.5g
Cholesterol	60mg
Sodium	440mg
Potassium	408mg
Total Carbohydrate	18g
Dietary Fiber	3g
Sugars	9g
Protein	20g

Nonstick cooking spray

1 1/2 pounds boneless pork chops, trimmed of fat and cut into 1-inch pieces

2 medium onions (8 ounces total), cut into 8 wedges each

1 1/2 cups frozen corn kernels, thawed

8-ounce can no-salt-added tomato sauce

1 tablespoon mild Louisiana hot sauce

1 teaspoon Worcestershire sauce

2 teaspoons smoked paprika

2 teaspoons ground cumin

2 teaspoons instant coffee granules, preferably espresso variety

1 tablespoon plus 1 teaspoon sugar

1/2 teaspoon dried thyme leaves

1/2 teaspoon garlic powder

1/2 teaspoon black pepper

3/4 teaspoon salt

1 tablespoon extra-virgin olive oil

1 **Coat a 3 1/2- to 4-quart slow cooker with cooking spray.** Place all the ingredients, except the oil, into the slow cooker. Stir to blend, cover and cook on high for 4 hours, or on low for 7 1/2–8 hours, or until pork is very tender. Stir in the oil.

2 **Serve in bowls.**

Roasted Tomato, Roasted Garlic White Beans

Makes 2 cups
Serves: 4
Serving Size: 1/2 cup

**Exchanges/
Food Choices:**
1 Starch
1 Vegetable
1 1/2 Fat

Calories	180
Calories from Fat	70
Total Fat	8g
Saturated Fat	2g
Trans Fat	0g
Monounsaturated Fat	3g
Cholesterol	5mg
Sodium	380mg
Potassium	505mg
Total Carbohydrate	22g
Dietary Fiber	8g
Sugars	4g
Protein	8g

Nonstick cooking spray

3 cups (1 1/2 pints) grape tomatoes, rinsed and patted dry

4 medium garlic cloves, peeled

4 teaspoons extra-virgin olive oil, divided

15-ounce can no-salt-added northern beans, rinsed and drained

1/4 teaspoon salt

1/4 cup chopped fresh basil leaves

1/2 cup crumbled reduced-fat feta cheese

1 **Coat a 6-quart slow cooker with cooking spray.** Place the tomatoes and garlic in the slow cooker and toss with 2 teaspoons oil. Cover and cook on high for 3 hours and 15 minutes, or on low for 6 1/2 hours, or until tomatoes are tender.

2 **Gently stir the beans and salt into the tomatoes in the slow cooker; drizzle with the remaining 2 teaspoons oil.** Cover and let stand 5 minutes to heat through.

3 **Sprinkle with the basil and feta.**

Cook's Note:
Serve over your choice of pasta, rice, or potatoes.

Grape Tomato and Kalamata Cod

Makes 3 cups
Serves: 4
Serving Size: 3/4 cup

**Exchanges/
Food Choices:**
2 Vegetable
2 Lean Meat
2 Fat

Calories	230
Calories from Fat	90
Total Fat	10g
Saturated Fat	2g
Trans Fat	0g
Monounsaturated Fat	5.5g
Cholesterol	40mg
Sodium	520mg
Potassium	679mg
Total Carbohydrate	13g
Dietary Fiber	3g
Sugars	8g
Protein	20g

Nonstick cooking spray

2 cups (1 pint) grape tomatoes, halved

1 cup diced onion

8-ounce can no-salt-added tomato sauce

2 tablespoons no-salt-added tomato paste

1/4 cup water

1/4 teaspoon dried pepper flakes

12 ounces cod fillets, cut into 1-inch chunks

1 tablespoon extra-virgin olive oil

1/4 cup finely chopped fresh basil leaves

16 pitted kalamata olives, coarsely chopped

1/8 teaspoon salt

1/4 cup grated Parmesan cheese

1 **Coat a 3 1/2- to 4-quart slow cooker with cooking spray.** Place the tomatoes, onions, tomato sauce, tomato paste, water, and pepper flakes in the slow cooker. Cover and cook on high for 3 1/2 hours, or on low for 7 hours, or until onions are tender.

2 **Stir in remaining ingredients, except the cheese.** Cover and cook on high for 15–20 minutes or until fish is opaque. Sprinkle with cheese.

Cook's Note:
Serve over your choice of pasta, rice, or potatoes.

Deep South Shrimp Stew

Makes 6 cups
Serves: 6
Serving Size: 1 cup

**Exchanges/
Food Choices:**
1/2 Starch
1 Vegetable
1 Lean Meat
1/2 Fat

Calories	150
Calories from Fat	30
Total Fat	3.5g
Saturated Fat	0.5g
Trans Fat	0g
Monounsaturated Fat	1.5g
Cholesterol	0mg
Sodium	450mg
Potassium	429mg
Total Carbohydrate	15g
Dietary Fiber	3g
Sugars	6g
Protein	14g

Nonstick cooking spray

8 ounces red potatoes, unpeeled and cut into 1-inch cubes

1 medium green bell pepper, seeded, stemmed, and cut into 1-inch pieces

1 cup coarsely chopped onion

1 medium celery stalk, sliced

14.5-ounce can no-salt-added stewed tomatoes

14.5-ounce can reduced-sodium chicken broth

1 teaspoon dried thyme leaves

1/2 teaspoon garlic powder

12 ounces raw medium shrimp, peeled

1/4 cup chopped fresh parsley

1 1/2 teaspoons seafood seasoning, such as Old Bay

1 teaspoon sugar, *optional*

1 tablespoon extra-virgin olive oil

1 **Coat a 3 1/2- to 4-quart slow cooker with cooking spray.** Place the potatoes, bell pepper, onions, celery, tomatoes, broth, thyme, and garlic powder in the slow cooker. Cover and cook on high for 3 hours, or on low for 5 1/2–6 hours, or until vegetables are tender.

2 **Stir in the shrimp, parsley, seafood seasoning, sugar, and oil.** Cover and cook on high 20 minutes.

3 **Turn off heat, uncover, and let stand 15 minutes to absorb flavors.**

Cook's Note:
Don't skip the last step. It's important to let the mixture stand uncovered for the flavors to penetrate.

Southern Shrimp Creole

Makes 6 cups
Serves: 6
Serving Size: 1 cup

**Exchanges/
Food Choices:**
3 Vegetable
1 Lean Meat
1/2 Fat

Calories	170
Calories from Fat	35
Total Fat	4g
Saturated Fat	0.5g
Trans Fat	0g
Monounsaturated Fat	1.5g
Cholesterol	0mg
Sodium	410mg
Potassium	394mg
Total Carbohydrate	15g
Dietary Fiber	4g
Sugars	7g
Protein	17g

Nonstick cooking spray

3 cups diced green bell pepper

1 1/2 cups diced onion

2 medium celery stalks, sliced

2 cups frozen cut okra, thawed

1 cup grape tomatoes, halved

8-ounce can no-salt-added tomato sauce

1/2 6-ounce can no-salt-added tomato paste

1 1/2 teaspoons dried thyme leaves

2 dried bay leaves

1 teaspoon garlic powder

1 tablespoon mild Louisiana hot sauce

1 pound raw medium shrimp, peeled

1/2 teaspoon salt

1/2 teaspoon black pepper

1/4 cup chopped fresh parsley

1 tablespoon extra-virgin olive oil

1 Coat a 3 1/2- to 4-quart slow cooker with cooking spray.

2 **Place the bell peppers, onions, celery, okra, tomatoes, tomato sauce, tomato paste, thyme, bay leaves, garlic powder, and hot sauce in the slow cooker.** Cover and cook on high for 4 hours, or on low for 8 hours, or until onions are tender.

3 **Add the remaining ingredients, cover, and cook on high 20 minutes or until shrimp are opaque in center.** Uncover and let stand 15 minutes to absorb flavors.

Cook's Note:
Freeze unused creole in 1-cup portions in airtight containers for up to 1 month.

Cumin Black Beans and Rice

Makes 4 cups beans and 2 cups rice
Serves: 6
Serving Size: 2/3 cup beans, 1/3 cup rice, and 2 tablespoons sour cream

Exchanges/ Food Choices:
2 Starch
1 Vegetable
1 Lean Meat

Calories	230
Calories from Fat	30
Total Fat	3.5g
Saturated Fat	0.5g
Trans Fat	0g
Monounsaturated Fat	1.5g
Cholesterol	5mg
Sodium	350mg
Potassium	677mg
Total Carbohydrate	43g
Dietary Fiber	10g
Sugars	9g
Protein	10g

1 cup dried black beans

3 cups water

Nonstick cooking spray

1 cup diced onion

1 cup diced red or green bell pepper

10-ounce can diced tomatoes with green chilies, such as Rotel

14.5-ounce can reduced-sodium vegetable broth or chicken broth

2 medium garlic cloves, minced

2 dried bay leaves

1 teaspoon dried oregano leaves

1 tablespoon extra-virgin olive oil

1 teaspoon ground cumin

1/4 teaspoon salt

10-ounce package frozen brown rice

3/4 cup fat-free sour cream

1 1/2 medium limes, cut into 6 wedges total

1 **Combine the beans and water in a bowl, cover, and let soak overnight.** Or place beans in a large saucepan and bring to a boil over high heat for 2 minutes. Turn off heat, cover, and let stand 1 hour.

2 **Drain beans, discarding water.** Coat a 3 1/2- to 4-quart slow cooker with cooking spray. Add the beans, onion, bell pepper, tomatoes, broth, garlic, bay leaves, and oregano. Cover and cook on high for 5 hours, or on low for 9–10 hours, or until beans are tender.

3 **Stir in the oil, cumin, and salt.**

4 **Prepare rice according to package directions, omitting any salt or fat.** Serve beans over the rice and top with sour cream and lime wedges.

Coconut Vegetable Curry

Makes 5 cups
Serves: 5
Serving Size: 1 cup

**Exchanges/
Food Choices:**
1/2 Starch
2 Vegetable
1/2 Fat

Calories	100
Calories from Fat	30
Total Fat	3g
Saturated Fat	2g
Trans Fat	0g
Monounsaturated Fat	0g
Cholesterol	0mg
Sodium	450mg
Potassium	393mg
Total Carbohydrate	16g
Dietary Fiber	4g
Sugars	5g
Protein	3g

Nonstick cooking spray

3 cups cauliflower florets

1 cup peeled, chopped sweet potato

1 cup diced onion

1 cup frozen cut green beans

15-ounce can no-salt-added garbanzo beans, rinsed and drained

2 cups no-salt-added vegetable broth

1 tablespoon curry powder

1/4 teaspoon cayenne pepper

1/2 13-ounce can light coconut milk

1/4 cup chopped fresh cilantro leaves

3/4 teaspoon salt

1 **Coat a 3 1/2- to 4-quart slow cooker with cooking spray.** Stir together the cauliflower, potatoes, onion, green beans, garbanzo beans, broth, curry, and cayenne in the slow cooker.

2 **Cover and cook on high for 2 1/2 hours, or on low for 5 hours, or until potatoes are tender.** Stir in the remaining ingredients.

Cook's Note:
This dish is even better the next day.

CHAPTER 6
Poultry Entrées

Simply Slow Roasted Chicken and Gravy

**Makes 18 ounces
cooked chicken and
1 1/2 cups gravy**
Serves: 6
Serving Size: 3 ounces
cooked chicken and 1/4 cup
gravy

**Exchanges/
Food Choices:**
4 Lean Meat
1/2 Fat

Calories	210
Calories from Fat	60
Total Fat	7g
Saturated Fat	1.5g
Trans Fat	0g
Monounsaturated Fat	3g
Cholesterol	100mg
Sodium	400mg
Potassium	354mg
Total Carbohydrate	4g
Dietary Fiber	1g
Sugars	1g
Protein	31g

Nonstick cooking spray

1 teaspoon paprika

2 teaspoons dried sage
or dried thyme leaves

1 teaspoon garlic powder

1/2 teaspoon coarsely
ground black pepper

3/4 teaspoon salt,
divided

1/2 medium (4-ounce)
onion, cut into 4 wedges

3 1/2–4-pound whole
chicken, cavity
cleaned, rinsed, and
patted dry

1 tablespoon extra-virgin
olive oil

2 tablespoons water

2 tablespoons cornstarch

1   **Lightly coat a 3 1/2- to 4-quart slow
cooker with cooking spray.**

2   **In a small bowl, stir together the
paprika, sage, garlic powder, black
pepper, and 1/2 teaspoon salt.** Place
the onion wedges in the cavity of the
chicken.

3   **Coat the chicken with the olive
oil and sprinkle the spice mixture
evenly over the chicken.** Place in
slow cooker, cover, and cook on high
for 1 hour; reduce heat and cook on
low for 3–3 1/2 hours or until the
internal temperature of the chicken
reaches 165°F when tested with a meat
thermometer.

4   **Remove the chicken with 2 large
spoons and place on cutting board.**
Remove and discard the onion
wedges. Let chicken stand on cutting
board 15 minutes before slicing.

5   **Meanwhile, place a zip-top plastic bag
inside a 2-cup glass measure.** Pour the
broth mixture into the bag. Let stand 2
minutes; the fat will rise to the top.

6   **Seal bag and carefully snip off one
bottom corner of bag.** Drain drippings
into measuring cup, stopping before
fat layer reaches opening; discard
remaining fat.

7   **In a medium saucepan, stir together
the water and cornstarch until the
cornstarch is completely dissolved.**
Stir in the broth mixture and remaining
1/4 teaspoon salt. Bring to a boil over
medium-high heat. Boil 2 minutes or
until thickened slightly. Serve with the
sliced chicken.

Cook's Note:
Be sure not to cook the chicken more than
4 1/2 hours or else the chicken breast will
become dry.

Saucy Herb Chicken Drumsticks

**Makes 8 drumsticks
and 1/2 cup sauce**
Serves: 4
Serving Size: 2 drumsticks
and 2 tablespoons sauce

**Exchanges/
Food Choices:**
3 Lean Meat

Calories	150
Calories from Fat	40
Total Fat	4.5g
Saturated Fat	1g
Trans Fat	0g
Monounsaturated Fat	1g
Cholesterol	95mg
Sodium	290mg
Potassium	295mg
Total Carbohydrate	1g
Dietary Fiber	0g
Sugars	0g
Protein	26g

Nonstick cooking spray

8 chicken drumsticks,
skin removed (about
2 pounds skinned)

1/3 cup reduced-sodium
chicken broth, divided

1/2 teaspoon garlic
powder

1/2 teaspoon dried sage
leaves, crushed

1/4 teaspoon dried thyme
leaves, crushed

1/4 teaspoon paprika

1/4 teaspoon salt

1/4 teaspoon black pepper

1 teaspoon cornstarch

2 tablespoons finely
chopped fresh parsley

1 **Lightly coat a 3 1/2- to 4-quart
slow cooker with cooking spray.** Put
the drumsticks in the slow cooker.
Pour 1/4 cup broth over chicken
and sprinkle evenly with the garlic,
sage, thyme, paprika, salt, and black
pepper.

2 **Cover and cook on high for 3 hours,
or on low for 6 hours, or until
chicken is no longer pink in center.**
Do not cook longer or the texture of
the chicken will not be as desirable.

3 **Remove drumsticks, place on a
serving platter, and cover to keep
warm.** Place a fine-mesh sieve over
a small saucepan. Pour the pan
drippings into the sieve, discarding
any solids.

4 **In a small bowl, stir together the
remaining broth and cornstarch
until cornstarch is completely
dissolved.** Stir the cornstarch
mixture into the pan drippings.
Bring to a boil over medium-high
heat and continue boiling 1 minute.
Pour the sauce over the chicken.
Top with parsley.

Cook's Note:
To remove the skin of the chicken drumsticks easily,
use paper towels to pull off the skin. They add a bit of
traction to keep your fingers from slipping.

Coconut Curry Chicken and Rice

Makes 7 1/2 cups
Serves: 6
Serving Size: 1 1/4 cups

**Exchanges/
Food Choices:**
1 Starch
1 Fruit
1 Vegetable
3 Lean Meat

Calories	310
Calories from Fat	60
Total Fat	7g
Saturated Fat	2.5g
Trans Fat	0g
Monounsaturated Fat	1g
Cholesterol	75mg
Sodium	490mg
Potassium	677mg
Total Carbohydrate	33g
Dietary Fiber	3g
Sugars	17g
Protein	27g

Nonstick cooking spray

1 cup diced onion

1 1/2 cups diced red bell pepper

4 medium garlic cloves, minced

8-ounce can pineapple tidbits in own juice, drained

1/3 cup raisins

14-ounce can reduced-sodium chicken broth

1 1/2 tablespoons curry powder, divided

2 12-ounce bone-in, skinless chicken breasts

1 cup uncooked instant brown rice

1 cup light coconut milk

1 tablespoon sugar

1–2 teaspoons grated gingerroot

1/2 teaspoon salt

1/4 cup chopped fresh cilantro leaves

1 **Coat a 3 1/2- to 4-quart slow cooker with cooking spray.** Stir together the onions, bell pepper, garlic, pineapple, raisins, broth, and 1 tablespoon curry powder in the slow cooker.

2 **Place the chicken breasts on top and sprinkle evenly with the remaining curry powder.** Cover and cook on high for 2 1/2–3 hours, or on low for 5–6 hours, or until chicken is no longer pink in center.

3 **Remove the chicken.** Gently stir in the rice. Cover and cook 15–20 minutes longer on high or until rice is tender.

4 **Meanwhile, remove the chicken from the bones, discard bones, and return the chicken to the rice mixture with the remaining ingredients, except the cilantro.** Serve sprinkled with cilantro.

Chicken Cheddar Rice with Asparagus

Makes 6 cups
Serves: 4
Serving Size: 1 1/4 cups

**Exchanges/
Food Choices:**
1 Starch
2 Vegetable
2 Lean Meat
1 Fat

Calories	260
Calories from Fat	80
Total Fat	8g
Saturated Fat	3.5g
Trans Fat	0g
Monounsaturated Fat	1.5g
Cholesterol	45mg
Sodium	460mg
Potassium	574mg
Total Carbohydrate	27g
Dietary Fiber	3g
Sugars	4g
Protein	17g

Nonstick cooking spray

2 cups water

8 ounces boneless, skinless, chicken thigh meat, trimmed of fat and cut into bite-size pieces

1 1/2 cups diced onion

1 cup uncooked brown rice, preferably parboiled variety

4 medium garlic cloves, minced

2 teaspoons sodium-free chicken bouillon granules

1/2 teaspoon dried thyme leaves

2 cups fresh asparagus tips, broken in 2-inch pieces, or frozen French cut green beans, thawed

1/2 teaspoon salt

2 ounces (1/2 cup) reduced-fat sharp Cheddar cheese, shredded

1 **Coat a 3 1/2- to 4-quart slow cooker with cooking spray.** Place the water, chicken, onion, rice, garlic, chicken bouillon, and thyme in the slow cooker. Cover and cook on high for 1 1/2 hours or on low for 3 hours.

2 **Turn off the heat.** Fluff the rice with a fork. Stir in the asparagus. Cover and let stand 10 minutes. Stir in the salt and sprinkle with the cheese.

Handwritten note at top: 2-2017 NO: DIDN'T LIKE MINUTE BROWN RICE

Chicken with Picante Rice

Makes 4 chicken breasts and 2 cups rice
Serves: 4
Serving Size: 3 ounces cooked chicken and 1/2 cup rice

**Exchanges/
Food Choices:**
1 1/2 Starch
3 Lean Meat
1/2 Fat

Calories	270
Calories from Fat	60
Total Fat	7g
Saturated Fat	3g
Trans Fat	0g
Monounsaturated Fat	1.5g
Cholesterol	75mg
Sodium	580mg
Potassiujm	249mg
Total Carbohydrate	21g
Dietary Fiber	2g
Sugars	2g
Protein	30g

Nonstick cooking spray

4 4-ounce boneless, skinless, chicken breasts, trimmed of fat

1/2 cup picante sauce

10-ounce package frozen brown rice *MINUTE*

1/4 cup water

1/4 teaspoon salt *OMIT*

1/4 cup chopped fresh cilantro leaves

1/2 cup shredded reduced-fat sharp Cheddar cheese

1 medium lime, quartered

1 **Coat a 3 1/2- to 4-quart slow cooker with cooking spray.** Place the chicken in the slow cooker in a single layer. Spoon the picante sauce over the chicken. Cover and cook on high for 1 1/2–2 hours, or 3–4 hours on low, or until chicken is no longer pink in the center.

2 **Turn the chicken over several times to remove any sauce from the chicken.** Remove chicken and set aside on separate plate. Stir the rice, water, and salt into the pan drippings in the slow cooker.

3 **Place the chicken on top of the rice mixture; sprinkle the cilantro and the cheese over the chicken.** Cover and cook on low 30 minutes. Serve with lime wedges.

Salsa Verde Mozzarella Chicken

Makes 4 chicken breasts and 2 cups rice
Serves: 4
Serving Size: 3 ounces cooked chicken and 1/2 cup rice

Exchanges/ Food Choices:
1 Starch
1 Vegetable
3 Lean Meat
1 Fat

Calories	290
Calories from Fat	80
Total Fat	10g
Saturated Fat	2.5g
Trans Fat	0g
Monounsaturated Fat	3g
Cholesterol	80mg
Sodium	590mg
Potassium	597mg
Total Carbohydrate	19g
Dietary Fiber	2g
Sugars	4g
Protein	29g

Nonstick cooking spray

4 4-ounce boneless, skinless, chicken breasts, trimmed of fat, rinsed and patted dry

1/2 teaspoon ground cumin

1/8 teaspoon cayenne pepper

7-ounce can salsa verde

1/4 cup water

3/4 cup uncooked instant brown rice

2 teaspoons extra-virgin olive oil

1/2 cup shredded part-skim mozzarella cheese

1/2 cup grape tomatoes, quartered

1 medium lime, cut into 4 wedges, *optional*

1 **Coat a 3 1/2- to 4-quart slow cooker with cooking spray.** Place chicken in the bottom of the slow cooker, sprinkle evenly with the cumin and cayenne, and pour the salsa verde evenly over all. Cover and cook on high for 2 hours, or on low for 4 hours, or until the chicken is no longer pink in the center.

2 **Remove the chicken pieces and set aside on a separate plate.** Cover to keep warm.

3 **Stir the rice, water, and oil into the remaining ingredients in the slow cooker.** Cover and cook on high 20 minutes or until the rice is tender.

4 **Turn off the heat.** Arrange the chicken on top of the rice, sprinkle with the cheese and tomatoes, cover, and let stand 5 minutes to allow the cheese to melt. Serve with lime wedges, if desired.

Chicken Pot Biscuits

Makes 3 cups chicken mixture and 4 biscuits
Serves: 4
Serving Size: 3/4 cup chicken mixture and 1 biscuit

Exchanges/ Food Choices:
3 Starch
1 Vegetable
3 Lean Meat
1/2 Fat

Calories	430
Calories from Fat	120
Total Fat	13g
Saturated Fat	3g
Trans Fat	0g
Monounsaturated Fat	3g
Cholesterol	70mg
Sodium	830mg
Potassium	805mg
Total Carbohydrate	45g
Dietary Fiber	4g
Sugars	5g
Protein	28g

FILLING
Nonstick cooking spray

8 ounces boneless, skinless, chicken thighs, trimmed of fat and cut into bite-size pieces

8 ounces boneless, skinless, chicken breast, cut into bite-size pieces

1 cup diced red bell pepper

1/2 cup diced onion

2 teaspoons sodium-free chicken bouillon granules

1/2 teaspoon poultry seasoning or dried sage

3/4 cup fat-free half-and-half

1 1/2 tablespoons reduced-fat biscuit and baking mix

1/4 teaspoon salt

1 cup frozen green peas

1 tablespoon trans-fat-free margarine

2 tablespoons finely chopped fresh parsley

BISCUITS
2/3 cup reduced-fat biscuit and baking mix

1/3 cup fat-free half-and-half

1   **Coat a 3 1/2- to 4-quart slow cooker with cooking spray.** Place the chicken, bell peppers, onions, bouillon granules, and poultry seasoning in the slow cooker. Cover and cook on high 2 hours, or on low 4 hours, or until chicken is no longer pink in center.

2   **In a small bowl, whisk together 3/4 cup half-and-half, 1 1/2 tablespoons baking mix, and the salt.** Stir into the slow cooker with the peas, margarine, and parsley. Cover and cook 15 minutes to thicken.

3   **Meanwhile, preheat the oven to 400°F.** In the same small bowl used to mix the half-and-half ingredients, stir together the remaining 2/3 cup baking mix and 1/3 cup half-and-half. Spoon 4 mounds onto a nonstick baking sheet coated with cooking spray. Bake 7 minutes or until slightly golden on edges.

4   **To serve, place equal amounts of the chicken mixture in shallow soup bowls; top each with a biscuit.**

Cook's Note:
This may be made without the biscuits and served over your choice of pasta, rice, or potatoes, if desired. Use all-purpose flour to thicken instead of the baking mix.

Pizza Pot Pasta

Makes about 5 1/3 cups
Serves: 4
Serving Size: about 1 1/3 cups

**Exchanges/
Food Choices:**
2 Starch
4 Lean Meat
1/2 Fat

Calories	370
Calories from Fat	80
Total Fat	9g
Saturated Fat	3g
Trans Fat	0g
Monounsaturated Fat	2g
Cholesterol	90mg
Sodium	460mg
Potassium	871mg
Total Carbohydrate	34g
Dietary Fiber	5g
Sugars	9g
Protein	35g

Nonstick cooking spray

1 pound boneless, skinless, chicken breast, trimmed of fat and cut into bite-size pieces

1/2 cup diced tomatoes, drained

2 tablespoons no-salt-added tomato paste

1 tablespoon dried basil leaves

4 ounces uncooked whole-grain penne or rotini

1 ounce turkey pepperoni slices, quartered

1 cup prepared low-sodium spaghetti sauce

1/3 cup shredded part-skim mozzarella cheese

4 teaspoons grated Parmesan cheese

1 **Coat a 3 1/2- to 4-quart slow cooker with cooking spray.** Combine the chicken, tomatoes, tomato paste, and basil in the slow cooker. Cover and cook on high for 1 hour and 15 minutes, or on low for 2 1/2 hours, or until chicken is no longer pink in center.

2 **Fifteen minutes before the chicken is done, cook the pasta according to package directions, omitting any salt or fats.** Drain well.

3 **Stir the pasta and pepperoni into the chicken mixture.** Spoon the spaghetti sauce over all. Sprinkle evenly with mozzarella and Parmesan cheese. Cover and cook on high for 15 minutes to absorb flavors and heat through.

Slow "Roasted" Herbed Turkey Breast

Makes about 3 pounds cooked turkey meat
Serves: 16
Serving Size: 3 ounces cooked turkey meat

Exchanges/ Food Choices:
5 Lean Meat
1 Fat

Calories	260
Calories from Fat	110
Total Fat	13g
Saturated Fat	3g
Trans Fat	0g
Monounsaturated Fat	5g
Cholesterol	100mg
Sodium	160mg
Potassium	427mg
Total Carbohydrate	1g
Dietary Fiber	0g
Sugars	0g
Protein	34g

Nonstick cooking spray

6-pound frozen whole bone-in turkey breast, thawed, rinsed, and patted dry

1/4 cup finely chopped fresh parsley

3 tablespoons Dijon mustard

2 tablespoons extra-virgin olive oil

1 1/2 teaspoons dried thyme leaves

1 teaspoon dried sage

1/2 teaspoon dried rosemary

1/2 teaspoon black pepper

1/8 teaspoon cayenne pepper

1/2 teaspoon paprika

1 **Coat a 6-quart slow cooker with cooking spray.** Place the turkey on a clean work surface. Carefully loosen skin from breast by inserting fingers between the skin and meat and gently pushing.

2 **In a small bowl, combine the remaining ingredients, except the paprika.** Place the parsley mixture under the skin and over the breast meat, being careful not to tear the skin. Sprinkle the paprika evenly over the turkey breast and rub evenly over all.

3 **Place the turkey in the slow cooker, breast side up.** Cover and cook on high for 1 hour. Reduce the heat and continue cooking on low for 4–5 hours or until a meat thermometer inserted in the thickest part of the breast registers 165°F.

4 **Place turkey on cutting board and let stand 20 minutes.** Carefully remove the skin, keeping the seasonings on the breast, and discard the skin; thinly slice.

Easy Italian Pan Meatloaf

Makes 1 meatloaf
Serves: 4
Serving Size: 1/4 meatloaf

**Exchanges/
Food Choices:**
1 Starch
3 Lean Meat
1 Fat

Calories	250
Calories from Fat	80
Total Fat	9g
Saturated Fat	2.5g
Trans Fat	0g
Monounsaturated Fat	0g
Cholesterol	65mg
Sodium	530mg
Potassium	242mg
Total Carbohydrate	15g
Dietary Fiber	2g
Sugars	5g
Protein	26g

Nonstick cooking spray

1 pound 93%-lean ground turkey

1/2 cup diced onion

1/4 cup quick-cooking oats

1/4 cup finely chopped fresh parsley

3/4 cup prepared low-sodium spaghetti sauce, divided

1 tablespoon dried basil leaves

1/2 1.25-ounce packet 30%-less-sodium meat loaf seasoning mix

2 egg whites

2 teaspoons grated Parmesan cheese

1 **Coat an 8 1/2 x 4 1/2 x 2 1/2-inch loaf pan with cooking spray.** Set aside.

2 **In a medium bowl, combine the turkey, onions, oats, parsley, 1/4 cup spaghetti sauce, basil, seasoning mix, and egg whites.** Do not overmix. Place in the loaf pan and lightly smooth the surface. Spoon the remaining 1/2 cup sauce over all.

3 **Place a small wire rack, or 3–4 foil balls made from sheets of foil about 12 x 6 inches, in the bottom of a 6-quart slow cooker.** Put the loaf pan on top. Cover and cook on high for 3 1/2 hours, or on low for 7 hours, or until a meat thermometer inserted into meatloaf reaches an internal temperature of 170°F.

4 **Turn off the heat, remove cover, and sprinkle with the cheese.** Let stand 10 minutes to absorb any liquid. Remove from the pan and slice.

POULTRY ENTRÉES POULTRY ENTRÉES POULTRY ENTRÉES POULTRY ENTRÉES POULTRY ENTRÉES **POULTRY ENTRÉES** POULTRY ENTRÉES POULTRY ENTRÉES

POULTRY

Italian Sausage-Stuffed Zucchini Boats

Makes 8 stuffed squash
Serves: 4
Serving Size: 2 squash

**Exchanges/
Food Choices:**
1/2 Starch
1 Vegetable
1 Medium-Fat Meat

Calories	130
Calories from Fat	45
Total Fat	5g
Saturated Fat	0g
Trans Fat	0g
Monounsaturated Fat	0g
Cholesterol	25mg
Sodium	590mg
Potassium	208mg
Total Carbohydrate	13g
Dietary Fiber	2g
Sugars	3g
Protein	9g

Nonstick cooking spray

4 medium zucchini squash, halved lengthwise

6 ounces hot Italian turkey sausage, casings removed

1/2 cup diced onion

1/2 10-ounce package frozen brown rice

1/4 cup finely chopped red bell pepper

2 tablespoons chopped fresh parsley

1/4 teaspoon salt

2 tablespoons water

4 teaspoons grated Parmesan cheese

1 **Coat a 6-quart slow cooker with cooking spray.** Place the zucchini on a clean work surface. Using a teaspoon, scrape out the seeds and just enough flesh to make a cavity for stuffing.

2 **Heat a large skillet coated with cooking spray over medium-high heat.** Cook the sausage 3 minutes, add the onions and the "meat" of the squash, and cook for 3–4 minutes, or until most of the moisture has absorbed, stirring frequently. Remove from the heat, stir in the rice, bell pepper, parsley, and salt.

3 **Stuff the squash with the rice mixture.** Pour the water in the slow cooker. Transfer the squash in a single layer in the slow cooker. Cook, covered, on high for 2 1/2 hours, or on low for 5 hours, or until squash is tender.

4 **Turn off the heat, sprinkle evenly with the cheese, and let stand, uncovered, 15 minutes to allow flavors to absorb.**

CHAPTER 7
Beef Entrées

Pub House Dark Roasted Chuck Roast

Makes 4 cups shredded beef mixture and 1 1/2 cups sauce

Serves: 8
Serving Size: 1/2 cup shredded beef mixture plus 3 tablespoons sauce

Exchanges/ Food Choices:
1/2 Carbohydrate
3 Lean Meat

Calories	170
Calories from Fat	4
Total Fat	4.5g
Saturated Fat	1.5g
Trans Fat	0g
Monounsaturated Fat	1.5g
Cholesterol	70mg
Sodium	230mg
Potassium	272mg
Total Carbohydrate	6g
Dietary Fiber	1g
Sugars	3g
Protein	23g

Nonstick cooking spray

1 1/2 cups diced onion

2 pounds trimmed, extra-lean boneless chuck roast

1/2 cup dry red wine

1 tablespoon sodium-free beef granules

1 tablespoon instant coffee granules

2 teaspoons sugar

1 teaspoon garlic powder

1 teaspoon onion powder

1 teaspoon dried oregano leaves

1/2 teaspoon salt

2 tablespoons steak sauce

1 tablespoon water

1 1/2 teaspoons cornstarch

1 **Lightly coat a 3 1/2- to 4-quart slow cooker with cooking spray.** Place the onions in the bottom of the slow cooker.

2 **Lightly coat a large skillet with cooking spray and place over medium-high heat until hot.** Brown the beef 2 minutes on each side. Place the beef on top of the onions.

3 **Combine the remaining ingredients, except the water and cornstarch, in a small bowl.** Pour the wine mixture over the beef. Cover and cook on high for 3 1/2 hours, or on low for 7 hours, or until beef is tender.

4 **Place the beef on a cutting board.** In a small bowl, combine the water and cornstarch and stir until cornstarch is completely dissolved. Stir into the onion mixture in the slow cooker. Roughly shred the beef and return to the slow cooker. Cover and cook on high 20 minutes to thicken.

Cook's Note:

When buying meat or poultry, it's often necessary to purchase more than the recipe calls for. The fat that is trimmed off of the meat or poultry can be significant and you could end up with less meat or poultry than you need for the recipe.

Hearty Beef on Baked Potatoes

Makes 4 potatoes and 2 cups beef mixture
Serves: 4
Serving Size: 1 potato, 1/2 cup beef mixture, 2 tablespoons sour cream, and 1 tablespoon green onion

Exchanges/ Food Choices:
2 Starch
1 Vegetable
3 Lean Meat

Calories	310
Calories from Fat	45
Total Fat	5g
Saturated Fat	2g
Trans Fat	0g
Monounsaturated Fat	1.5g
Cholesterol	70mg
Sodium	470mg
Potassium	1186mg
Total Carbohydrate	39g
Dietary Fiber	3g
Sugars	6g
Protein	29g

Nonstick cooking spray

1 pound trimmed, extra-lean boneless chuck, cut into bite-size pieces

4 ounces whole mushrooms, quartered

1/2 cup diced onion

1/3 cup water

1/2 1.5-ounce packet Beef Stroganoff seasoning

4 medium red potatoes (6 ounces each), pierced in several areas with a fork

1/2 cup fat-free sour cream

1/4 cup finely chopped green onion

1. **Coat a 3 1/2- to 4-quart slow cooker with cooking spray.** Stir together the beef, mushrooms, onion, water, and seasoning packet in the slow cooker.

2. **Wrap each potato in aluminum foil and place directly on top of the beef mixture.** Cover and cook on high for 3 hours, or on low for 6 hours, or until potatoes are tender when pierced with a fork.

3. **Turn off the heat.** Remove potatoes, cut in half lengthwise, fluff the potatoes with a fork, and spoon equal amounts of the beef mixture on top of each potato. Top each with an equal amount of sour cream and green onion.

BEEF ENT

BEEF ENTRÉES · BEEF ENTRÉES · BEEF ENTRÉES · BEEF ENTRÉES · BEEF ENTRÉES · BEEF ENTRÉES · BEEF ENTRÉES · BEEF ENTRÉES · BEEF ENTRÉES · BEEF

BEEF

Beer-Braised Beef Brisket

Makes 1 1/2 pounds cooked beef, 4 cups sauce, and 4 cups cooked noodles

Serves: 8
Serving Size: about 3 ounces cooked beef, 1/2 cup sauce, and 1/2 cup cooked noodles

**Exchanges/
Food Choices:**
1 Starch
1/2 Fat

Calories	300
Calories from Fat	50
Total Fat	6g
Saturated Fat	1.5g
Trans Fat	0g
Monounsaturated Fat	1.5g
Cholesterol	95mg
Sodium	440mg
Potassium	712mg
Total Carbohydrate	30g
Dietary Fiber	4g
Sugars	8g
Protein	30g

Nonstick cooking spray

2 pounds lean beef brisket, trimmed of fat

12 ounces light beer, divided

2 cups diced green pepper

1 cup diced onion

4 ounces sliced mushrooms

8-ounce can no-salt-added tomato sauce

1/2 6-ounce can no-salt-added tomato paste

1/4 cup ketchup

1 tablespoon Worcestershire sauce

2 teaspoons balsamic vinegar

1 teaspoon coarsely ground black pepper

3/4 teaspoon salt

8 ounces uncooked whole-grain egg noodles

1 **Lightly coat a 3 1/2- to 4-quart slow cooker with cooking spray.**

2 **Lightly coat a large skillet with cooking spray and place over medium-high heat until hot.** Brown the beef 2 minutes on each side. Place in the slow cooker.

3 **Add 1/2 cup beer to the skillet and scrape to remove any browned bits.** Pour over the beef in slow cooker. Top with the peppers, onions, and mushrooms.

4 **Combine the remaining ingredients, except the noodles, in a large bowl. Stir until well blended** and add to the slow cooker. Cover and cook on high for 5 hours, or on low for 10 hours, or until beef is very tender.

5 **Place beef on cutting board and let stand 15 minutes.** Meanwhile, uncover the slow cooker and let stand to thicken slightly.

6 **Cook noodles according to package directions, omitting any salt or fats.** Serve beef mixture over cooked noodles.

Cook's Note:
May freeze leftovers in an airtight container, if desired.

Sweet Swiss Steaks

Makes 12 ounces cooked beef, 3 cups vegetable mixture, and 2 cups cooked pasta
Serves: 4
Serving Size: 3 ounces cooked beef, 3/4 cup vegetable mixture, and 1/2 cup cooked pasta

Exchanges/ Food Choices:
1 1/2 Starch
2 Vegetable
3 Lean Meat
1 Fat

Calories	340
Calories from Fat	100
Total Fat	11g
Saturated Fat	3.5g
Trans Fat	0g
Monounsaturated Fat	4g
Cholesterol	75mg
Sodium	470mg
Potassium	629mg
Total Carbohydrate	31g
Dietary Fiber	4g
Sugars	8g
Protein	31g

Nonstick cooking spray

1 cup (4 ounces) thinly sliced onion

1 large green bell pepper, seeded and thinly sliced

6 ounces sliced mushrooms

1 pound top round steak, trimmed of fat and cut into 4 pieces

8-ounce can no-salt-added tomato sauce

1 1/2 tablespoons steak sauce

1 tablespoon cider vinegar

1/2 teaspoon black pepper

4 ounces uncooked whole-grain rotini pasta

2 tablespoons trans-fat-free margarine

1/2 teaspoon salt

1 **Coat a 3 1/2- to 4-quart slow cooker with cooking spray.** Place onions, bell peppers, and mushrooms in the bottom of the slow cooker.

2 **Heat a large skillet coated with cooking spray over medum-high heat.** Brown the steaks, on one side only, for 3 minutes. Place on top of the vegetables, browned side up.

3 **Remove the skillet from the heat, stir in the tomato sauce, steak sauce, vinegar, and black pepper.** Stir bottom and sides to pick up any browned bits. Pour over the steaks. Cover and cook on low only for 5 1/2 hours or until tender.

4 **About 20 minutes before serving, prepare the pasta according to package directions, omitting any salt or fats.** Turn off heat, gently remove the steaks with a slotted spoon or spatula, and place on separate plate. Cover to keep warm.

5 **Stir the margarine and salt into the ingredients in the slow cooker.** Let stand, uncovered, 15 minutes to thicken slightly and absorb flavors. Drain pasta well, top with the beef slices, and spoon the vegetable mixture over beef.

Cook's Note:
Don't skip the last step; it's important to let stand for peak flavors and texture.

Cube Steak with Mushrooms and Gravy

Makes 4 cube steaks and about 2 cups mushroom mixture
Serves: 4
Serving Size: 3 ounces cooked beef and about 1/2 cup mushroom mixture

**Exchanges/
Food Choices:**
1/2 Carbohydrate
5 Lean Meat
1/2 Fat

Calories	280
Calories from Fat	70
Total Fat	8g
Saturated Fat	2.5g
Trans Fat	0g
Monounsaturated Fat	3.5g
Cholesterol	95mg
Sodium	220mg
Potassium	971mg
Total Carbohydrate	10g
Dietary Fiber	1g
Sugars	5g
Protein	39g

Nonstick cooking spray

1 cup diced onion

4 ounces sliced mushrooms

1 teaspoon canola oil

4 4-ounce cube steaks

1/4 cup water

1 tablespoon sodium-free beef bouillon

1 teaspoon salt-free steak grilling blend

1/2 cup fat-free milk

1 tablespoon all-purpose flour

1 teaspoon Worcestershire sauce

1/2 teaspoon salt

1/4 cup finely chopped green onion, *optional*

1 **Coat a 3 1/2- to 4-quart slow cooker with cooking spray.** Place onions and mushrooms in the bottom of the slow cooker.

2 **Heat the oil in a large skillet over medum-high heat.** Tilt the skillet to coat the bottom lightly. Brown the steaks on one side only for 4 minutes. Place on top of the vegetables, browned side up, overlapping slightly.

3 **Remove the skillet from the heat, add the water.** Stir bottom and sides to pick up any browned bits. Pour over the steaks.

4 **Sprinkle the steaks evenly with the bouillon granules and steak grilling blend.** Cover and cook on high for 2–2 1/2 hours, or on low for 4–5 hours, or until tender.

5 **Remove steaks and place on serving platter.** Cover to keep warm.

6 **In a small bowl, whisk together the milk, flour, Worcestershire, and salt until smooth.** Stir into the mushroom mixture, cover, and cook 15 minutes. Spoon over the steaks and sprinkle with the green onions.

Meatloaf on a Sling

[handwritten: 1-2017 GOOD]

Makes 1 meatloaf
Serves: 4
Serving Size: 1/4 meatloaf

**Exchanges/
Food Choices:**
1 1/2 Carbohydrate
3 Lean Meat

*[handwritten: * 1 SMIDGEN SPOON SWEET LEAF]*
*[handwritten: * 1 SMIDGEN SPOON GARLIC POWDER]*

Calories	240
Calories from Fat	50
Total Fat	6g
Saturated Fat	1.5g
Trans Fat	0g
Monounsaturated Fat	2g
Cholesterol	60mg
Sodium	450mg
Potassium	123mg
Total Carbohydrate	21g
Dietary Fiber	4g
Sugars	8g
Protein	27g

Nonstick cooking spray *[handwritten: 1/4 cup. FOR THE TOP]*

1/3 cup ketchup *[handwritten: + 1 TBS.]*

1 tablespoon water *[handwritten: + 1 tsp.]*

2 teaspoons Worcestershire sauce

1 pound extra-lean ground beef

3/4 cup diced green bell pepper *[handwritten: USED FROZEN]*

1/2 cup finely chopped onion

2/3 cup quick-cooking oats *[handwritten: MUST USE]*

2 tablespoons ground flaxseed *[handwritten: DIDN'T HAVE]*

1/4 cup egg substitute *[handwritten: OR 1 EGG]*

1/8 teaspoon cayenne, optional *[handwritten: DIDN'T USE]*

1/8 teaspoon salt *[handwritten: OMITED]*
[handwritten: 2 GARLIC CLOVES - MINCED]

3 18-inch sheets aluminum foil
[handwritten: 2 TB. FAT FREE MILK]

*[handwritten: * MIX MEAT INGRED.
COOK the NEXT DAY
FLAVORS to MIX]*

1. **Lightly coat a 3 1/2- to 4-quart slow cooker with cooking spray.**

2. **Combine the ketchup, water, and Worcestershire sauce in a small bowl.**

3. **Combine the beef, bell peppers, onions, oats, flaxseed, egg substitute, cayenne, salt, and 3 tablespoons of ketchup mixture in a medium bowl.** Shape into a loaf about 4 x 6 x 2 inches. Store remaining ketchup mixture in the refrigerator until needed.

4. **Fold each of the foil sheets in half lengthwise; coat the foil strips with cooking spray.** Crisscross the strips in a spoke-like fashion to act as a sling. Place the loaf in the center of the spokes.

5. **Lift the ends of the foil strips to transfer the loaf to the cooker, leaving the foil in place during cooking.** Cover and cook on low for 5 hours, or on high for 2 1/2 hours, or until internal temperature of meatloaf reaches 160°F.

6. **Turn off the slow cooker.** Spoon the remaining ketchup mixture evenly over the top of the meatloaf. Let stand, uncovered, 15 minutes to absorb flavors and for easier handling. Remove the meatloaf by lifting the loaf with the foil strips from the cooker.

BEEF

One-Pot Comfort Shepherd's Pie

Makes 6 cups
Serves: 1
Serving Size: 1 1/2 cups

**Exchanges/
Food Choices:**
1 1/2 Starch
2 Vegetable
3 Lean Meat
1 Fat

Calories	340
Calories from Fat	80
Total Fat	9g
Saturated Fat	3.5g
Trans Fat	0.5g
Monounsaturated Fat	3g
Cholesterol	65mg
Sodium	730mg
Potassium	427mg
Total Carbohydrate	34g
Dietary Fiber	4g
Sugars	11g
Protein	30g

Cook's Note:
When buying potato flakes, be sure to purchase brands that do not contain hydrogenated ingredients.

FILLING
Nonstick cooking spray

1 1/2 cups diced onion

1 pound extra-lean ground beef

1 tablespoon cornstarch

1/2 cup water

2 tablespoons no-salt-added tomato paste

1 tablespoon chili powder

1 teaspoon Worcestershire sauce

1/2 teaspoon salt

1 1/2 cups frozen mixed vegetables, thawed

TOPPING
1 1/3 cups water

2 tablespoons trans-fat-free margarine

1/4 teaspoon salt

1 1/3 cups instant potato flakes

1 1/4 cups fat-free milk

1/4 cup shredded reduced-fat sharp Cheddar cheese

1 **Coat a 3 1/2- to 4-quart slow cooker with cooking spray.**

2 **Heat a large skillet coated with cooking spray over medium-high heat.** Add onions, cook 2 minutes, stirring occasionally. Add ground beef, cook 4 minutes or until browned, stirring occasionally.

3 **Meanwhile, in a small bowl, whisk together the cornstarch and water until cornstarch is completely dissolved.** Stir the cornstarch mixture into the beef mixture and bring to a boil over medium-high heat. Place mixture in slow cooker with the tomato paste, chili powder, Worcestershire sauce, and 1/2 teaspoon salt. Top with the mixed vegetables.

4 **In the same skillet, prepare topping.** Combine remaining 1 1/3 cups water with the margarine and 1/4 teaspoon salt in the skillet and bring to a boil over medium-high heat.

5 **Remove skillet from heat; stir in the potato flakes and milk until blended.** Spoon the potatoes on top of the vegetables, spread evenly over all. Cover and cook on low only for 3 hours.

6 **Turn off heat and sprinkle with cheese.** Let stand 15 minutes, uncovered, to absorb liquid and thicken slightly.

Family Table Tamale Pie

Makes 9 cups
Serves: 6
Serving Size: 1 1/2 cups

**Exchanges/
Food Choices:**
2 1/2 Starch
1 Vegetable
2 Lean Meat
1 Fat

Calories	360
Calories from Fat	90
Total Fat	10g
Saturated Fat	3g
Trans Fat	0g
Monounsaturated Fat	4g
Cholesterol	45mg
Sodium	890mg
Potassium	386mg
Total Carbohydrate	46g
Dietary Fiber	9g
Sugars	13g
Protein	25g

Nonstick cooking spray

1 pound extra-lean ground beef

1 cup diced green bell pepper

15-ounce can no-salt-added black beans, rinsed and drained

14.5-ounce can no-salt-added diced tomatoes

4-ounce can chopped mild green chilies

1 1/2 tablespoons chili powder

1 tablespoon ground cumin

1/2 teaspoon salt

1 teaspoon Worcestershire sauce

8.5-ounce box corn muffin mix

2 egg whites

1/2 cup fat-free milk

1/4 cup shredded reduced-fat sharp Cheddar cheese

1 **Coat a 6-quart slow cooker with cooking spray.**

2 **Heat a large skillet coated with cooking spray over medium-high heat.** Brown the beef and place in the slow cooker with the bell pepper, beans, tomatoes, green chilies, chili powder, cumin, salt, and Worcestershire sauce. Stir until well blended.

3 **In a medium bowl, combine the muffin mix with the egg whites and milk.** Stir until just blended and spoon over the beef mixture, leaving a 1/2-inch border between the corn muffin mixture and the slow cooker.

4 **Cover and cook on high for 2 hours and 15 minutes, or on low for 4 1/2 hours, or until wooden pick inserted comes out clean.**

5 **Turn off the heat, sprinkle with the cheese, and let stand, uncovered, 20 minutes to absorb liquid and thicken slightly.**

Herbed Meatballs and Spaghetti Sauce

**Makes 24 meatballs
and 4 cups sauce**
Serves: 8
Serving Size: 3 meatballs
and 1/2 cup sauce

**Exchanges/
Food Choices:**
2 Starch
1 Lean Meat
1/2 Fat

Calories	230
Calories from Fat	60
Total Fat	7g
Saturated Fat	1.5g
Trans Fat	0g
Monounsaturated Fat	1.5g
Cholesterol	30mg
Sodium	210mg
Potassium	491mg
Total Carbohydrate	27g
Dietary Fiber	5g
Sugars	15g
Protein	15g

Nonstick cooking spray

12 ounces extra-lean
ground beef

3.5-ounce Italian turkey
sausage link, casing
removed

2/3 cup quick-cooking
oats

1/2 cup finely chopped
fresh parsley

1/2 cup egg substitute

1 1/2 tablespoons dried
basil leaves

1 teaspoon dried
rosemary

1/2 teaspoon dried fennel,
optional

1 teaspoon garlic power

1/4–1/2 teaspoon dried
pepper flakes

4 cups prepared spaghetti
sauce

1 cup water

1 1/2 tablespoons sugar

1 **Lightly coat a 3 1/2- to 4-quart
slow cooker with cooking spray.**

2 **Combine the ground beef, sausage,
oats, parsley, egg substitute, basil,
rosemary, fennel, garlic, and pepper
flakes in a medium bowl.** Shape into
24 balls.

3 **Combine the spaghetti sauce,
water, and sugar in another
medium bowl.**

4 **Lightly coat a large nonstick skillet
with cooking spray and place over
medium-high heat until hot.** Brown
the meatballs on all sides; place in
slow cooker. Pour the sauce mixture
evenly over all.

5 **Cover and cook on high for 3 hours
or on low for 6 hours.**

Cook's Note:
Serve over whole-grain pasta, as
open-face meatball sandwiches
using whole-grain Italian bread, or
freeze for later use.

Browned Gravy Meatballs

**Makes 32 meatballs and
1/2 cup gravy**
Serves: 4
Serving Size: 8 meatballs
and 1/8 cup gravy

**Exchanges/
Food Choices:**
1 Starch
4 Lean Meat
1 Fat

Calories	290
Calories from Fat	100
Total Fat	11g
Saturated Fat	2.5g
Trans Fat	0g
Monounsaturated Fat	5.5g
Cholesterol	60mg
Sodium	530mg
Potassium	526mg
Total Carbohydrate	18g
Dietary Fiber	2g
Sugars	3g
Protein	29g

MEATBALLS
Nonstick cooking spray

1 pound extra-lean ground
beef

2/3 cup finely chopped
green onion

2/3 cup quick-cooking oats

4 egg whites

1 teaspoon garlic powder

1 teaspoon dried oregano
leaves

1 teaspoon Worcestershire
sauce

1 tablespoon Dijon mustard

1/2 teaspoon black pepper

1/8 teaspoon cayenne

GRAVY
1 1/4 cups hot water,
divided

1 1/2 tablespoons all-
purpose flour

1 1/2 teaspoons sodium-
free beef granules

1 teaspoon instant coffee
granules, preferably
espresso variety

1/2 teaspoon salt

1 1/2 tablespoons extra-
virgin olive oil

1/2 teaspoon
Worcestershire sauce

1. **Coat a 6-quart slow cooker with
cooking spray.**

2. **In a medium bowl, combine the
meatball ingredients.** Shape into
32 meatballs.

3. **Heat a large skillet coated with
cooking spray over medium-high
heat.** Brown meatballs 4 minutes,
turning occasionally. Place in the
slow cooker in a single layer, cover,
and cook on high for 2 1/2 hours, or
on low for 5 hours, or until no longer
pink in center.

4. **In a small bowl, stir together
1/4 cup water and the flour.** Add to
the slow cooker with the remaining
1 cup water and the rest of the gravy
ingredients; gently stir until well
blended. Cover and cook on high
15 minutes to thicken.

Cook's Note:
Use two utensils, such as a
fork and tablespoon, to turn
meatballs easily.

BEEF ENT
BEEF ENTRÉES
BEEF ENTRÉES
BEEF
BEEF
BEEF ENTRÉES
BEEF ENTRÉES
BEEF ENTRÉES
BEEF ENTRÉES

CHAPTER 8

Pork Entrées

Pork Tenderloin with Deep-Spiced Reduction

Makes 12 ounces cooked pork and 1/4 cup sauce
Serves: 4
Serving Size: 3 ounces cooked pork and 1 tablespoon sauce

Exchanges/ Food Choices:
3 Lean Meat

Calories	130
Calories from Fat	25
Total Fat	2.5g
Saturated Fat	1g
Trans Fat	0g
Monounsaturated Fat	0.5g
Cholesterol	75mg
Sodium	220mg
Potassium	483mg
Total Carbohydrate	2g
Dietary Fiber	1g
Sugars	0g
Protein	24g

Nonstick cooking spray

1 1/2 teaspoons chili powder

1 teaspoon onion powder

1/2 teaspoon garlic powder

1/8–1/4 teaspoon ground cinnamon

1/4 teaspoon salt

1/2 teaspoon coarsely ground black pepper

1 pound pork tenderloin

1/4 cup water

1 **Lightly coat a 3 1/2- to 4-quart slow cooker with cooking spray.**

2 **In a small bowl, stir together the chili powder, onion powder, garlic powder, cinnamon, salt, and black pepper.** Sprinkle the mixture evenly over the pork and press down to adhere.

3 **Coat a large skillet with cooking spray and place over medium-high heat until hot.** Cook the pork for 2 minutes, turn and cook 2 more minutes or until browned. Remove the skillet from the heat.

4 **Transfer the pork to the slow cooker.** Pour the water in the skillet, scraping the bottom and sides to remove any browned bits, and pour around the pork.

5 **Cook, covered, on low for 2–2 1/2 hours, or on high for 1 hour and 15 minutes, or until the internal temperature of the pork registers 150°F on a meat thermometer.** Transfer to a cutting board. Let stand for about 5 minutes before slicing.

6 **Place a fine-mesh sieve over a large skillet.** Pour the pan drippings into the sieve, discarding any solids. Bring to a boil over medium-high heat. Continue boiling 1 minute or until the liquid measures 1/4 cup. Slice pork, and spoon sauce over all.

Cook's Note:
The pork will continue to cook during the standing time, reaching about 160°F. It should be a little pink in the center.

Spiced Pork Tenderloin with Soy-Ginger Sauce

2 pc of pork   *cook on the STOVE*

Makes 12 ounces cooked pork and about 3/4 cup sauce
Serves: 4
Serving Size: 3 ounces cooked pork and about 3 tablespoons sauce

Exchanges/ Food Choices:
3 Lean Meat
1/2 Fat

Calories	180
Calories from Fat	35
Total Fat	3.5g
Saturated Fat	1g
Trans Fat	0g
Monounsaturated Fat	1.5g
Cholesterol	75mg
Sodium	390mg
Potassium	483mg
Total Carbohydrate	3g
Dietary Fiber	0g
Sugars	1g
Protein	25g

Nonstick cooking spray

1/2 teaspoon ground cinnamon

1/4 teaspoon ground allspice

1/8 teaspoon dried pepper flakes

1/8 teaspoon salt

1 pound pork tenderloin

1 teaspoon canola oil

1/4 cup water

2 tablespoons light soy sauce

2 tablespoons cider vinegar

2 teaspoons cornstarch

2 tablespoons packed brown sugar substitute blend, such as Splenda

1–2 teaspoons grated gingerroot

1   **Coat a 3 1/2- to 4-quart slow cooker with cooking spray.**

2   **In a small bowl, combine the cinnamon, allspice, pepper flakes, and salt.** Sprinkle evenly over the pork and press down with fingertips to adhere.

3   **Heat the oil in a large skillet over medium-high heat.** Tilt skillet to coat bottom lightly. Brown the pork 1 1/2 minutes, turn, and cook 1 1/2 additional minutes. Remove the skillet from heat.

4   **Place pork in slow cooker.** Add the water and soy sauce to the skillet, scraping bottom and sides to release any browned bits. Pour over the pork, cover, and cook on high for 1 hour and 15 minutes, or on low for 2 1/2 hours, or until meat thermometer inserted into pork registers 145°F.

5   **Place pork on cutting board.** In a small bowl, stir together the vinegar and cornstarch until cornstarch is completely dissolved. Stir into the pan drippings in the slow cooker with the sugar substitute. Cover and cook on high 15 minutes or until thickened.

6   **Thinly slice the pork, stir the ginger into the slow cooker, and spoon sauce over pork.**

Rosemary "Roasted" Pork and New Potatoes

Makes 1 1/2 pounds cooked pork, 5 1/3 cups potatoes, and 1/2 cup juices
Serves: 8
Serving Size: about 3 ounces cooked pork, 2/3 cup potatoes, and 1 tablespoon juices

Exchanges/ Food Choices:
1/2 Starch
3 Lean Meat
1 Fat

Calories	220
Calories from Fat	90
Total Fat	11g
Saturated Fat	2g
Trans Fat	0g
Monounsaturated Fat	4.5g
Cholesterol	60mg
Sodium	460mg
Potassium	257mg
Total Carbohydrate	10g
Dietary Fiber	2g
Sugars	0g
Protein	19g

Nonstick cooking spray

2 pounds new potatoes, quartered

2 tablespoons extra-virgin olive oil, divided

2 pounds boneless, extra-lean pork loin, trimmed of fat

2 teaspoons onion powder

1 teaspoon garlic powder

1 teaspoon paprika

1/2–3/4 teaspoon dried rosemary

1/2 teaspoon black pepper

1/2 teaspoon salt, divided

1/4 cup water

1 **Coat a 6-quart slow cooker with cooking spray.**

2 **Place the potatoes on the bottom of the slow cooker.** Drizzle 1 tablespoon oil over the potatoes. Place the pork on top of the potatoes. Drizzle remaining tablespoon oil over the pork.

3 **In a small bowl, combine the onion powder, garlic powder, paprika, rosemary, black pepper, and 1/4 teaspoon salt.** Sprinkle evenly over the pork. Cover and cook on high for 2 1/2 hours, or on low for 5 hours, or until a meat thermometer inserted into pork registers 145°F.

4 **Remove pork from slow cooker and place on cutting board.** Cover pork with a tent of foil to keep warm. Continue to cook the remaining ingredients on high, covered, for 45 minutes or until potatoes are tender.

5 **After the pork has rested at least 30 minutes, thinly slice pork and cover to keep warm.** Remove potatoes with a slotted spoon and arrange around the pork.

6 **Stir the water and remaining 1/4 teaspoon salt into the pan residue in the slow cooker.** Stir, scraping the bottom and sides to remove any browned bits. Strain the pan residue through a fine-mesh strainer over a medium bowl. Pour the strained juices evenly over the pork.

Pineapple-Green Pepper Pork Chops

**Makes 4 pork chops,
2 cups sauce, and
2 cups rice**
Serves: 4
Serving Size: 3 ounces
cooked pork, 1/2 cup sauce,
and 1/2 cup rice

**Exchanges/
Food Choices:**
1 1/2 Starch
1/2 Fruit
3 Lean Meat
1/2 Fat

Calories	320
Calories from Fat	70
Total Fat	8g
Saturated Fat	2g
Trans Fat	0g
Monounsaturated Fat	2g
Cholesterol	60mg
Sodium	490mg
Potassium	414mg
Total Carbohydrate	32g
Dietary Fiber	2g
Sugars	12g
Protein	22g

Nonstick cooking spray

1 medium green bell
pepper, thinly sliced

4 4-ounce boneless pork
chops, trimmed of fat

3 tablespoons light soy
sauce

1 tablespoon ketchup

1 tablespoon balsamic
vinegar

1 teaspoon grated
gingerroot

1/8 teaspoon dried pepper
flakes

10-ounce package frozen
brown rice

8-ounce can crushed
pineapple in own juice

2 tablespoons packed
dark brown sugar
substitute blend, such as
Splenda

1 1/2 tablespoons
cornstarch

1/4 cup chopped fresh
cilantro leaves

1 **Coat a 3 1/2- to 4-quart slow
cooker with cooking spray.** Place
the bell peppers on the bottom of
the slow cooker. Top with the pork
chops.

2 **In a small bowl, whisk together
the soy sauce, ketchup, vinegar,
gingerroot, and pepper flakes.**
Spoon evenly over the pork. Cover
and cook on high for 2 1/2 hours, or
on low for 5 hours, or until pork is
tender.

3 **About 10 minutes before serving,
cook the rice according to package
directions.** Place on serving platter.
Place the pork chops on top of the
rice; cover to keep warm.

4 **In a small bowl, stir together
the pineapple and its juice, the
brown sugar substitute, and the
cornstarch.** Stir until cornstarch is
completely dissolved.

5 **Stir into the bell pepper mixture
in the slow cooker.** Cover and cook
on high for 15 minutes or until
thickened. Spoon over the pork and
sprinkle with the cilantro.

Cook's Note:
For a thicker consistency, mix 2 tablespoons water with an
additional 1 1/2–2 teaspoons cornstarch. Cover and cook
5 minutes longer on high.

PORK ENTRÉES   PORK ENTRÉES   PORK   ENTRÉES   PORK ENTRÉES   PORK ENT   PORK ENTRÉES   PORK ENT   PORK ENTRÉES   **PORK ENTRÉES**   PORK ENTRÉES

PORK

Oh-So-Tender Pork Chops and Gravy

Makes 4 pork chops and about 1 1/3 cups onion mixture
Serves: 4
Serving Size: 3 ounces cooked pork and about 1/3 cup onion mixture

Exchanges/ Food Choices:
1 Vegetable
3 Lean Meat
1 Fat

Calories	210
Calories from Fat	100
Total Fat	11g
Saturated Fat	2g
Trans Fat	0g
Monounsaturated Fat	4g
Cholesterol	60mg
Sodium	210mg
Potassium	629mg
Total Carbohydrate	7g
Dietary Fiber	1g
Sugars	3g
Protein	20g

Nonstick cooking spray

1 tablespoon canola oil

2 cups (8 ounces) thinly sliced onion

1/4 cup water

4 4-ounce boneless pork chops, trimmed of fat

2 teaspoons sodium-free beef bouillon granules

3/4 teaspoon black pepper

1/2 teaspoon paprika

1/2 teaspoon dried thyme leaves

1/2 teaspoon garlic powder

1/4 teaspoon salt

1 **Coat a 3 1/2- to 4-quart slow cooker with cooking spray.**

2 **Heat the oil in a large skillet over medium-high heat.** Cook onions 6 minutes or until richly browned, stirring occasionally. Add the water to the onions, stir, scraping bottom and sides to remove any browned bits; place in the slow cooker, and top with pork chops. Gently push the pork chops down into the onion mixture.

3 **In a small bowl, combine the remaining ingredients, except the salt, and sprinkle evenly over the pork chops.** Cover and cook on low only for 5 hours or until pork chops are very tender.

4 **Carefully remove the pork chops.** Stir the salt into the onion mixture and spoon onions over all.

Cook's Note:
Be sure to cook the onions to a rich brown; this is what gives the dish "character."

Home-Style Pork and Cheddar Casserole

Makes 4 cups
Serves: 4
Serving Size: 1 cup

**Exchanges/
Food Choices:**
1 Starch
1 Vegetable
2 Lean Meat
1 1/2 Fat

Calories	250
Calories from Fat	100
Total Fat	11g
Saturated Fat	2.5g
Trans Fat	0g
Monounsaturated Fat	3.5g
Cholesterol	50mg
Sodium	400mg
Potassium	771mg
Total Carbohydrate	19g
Dietary Fiber	2g
Sugars	3g
Protein	18g

Nonstick cooking spray

1 cup diced onion

2/3 cup uncooked brown rice, preferably parboiled variety

1 cup water

12 ounces boneless pork chops, trimmed of fat

1 tablespoon sodium-free beef bouillon granules

1/2 teaspoon instant coffee granules, preferably espresso variety

3/4 teaspoon dried thyme leaves

1/2 teaspoon black pepper

1 cup grape tomatoes, quartered

1 tablespoon canola oil

1/2 teaspoon salt

1/4 cup reduced-fat sharp Cheddar cheese, shredded (1 ounce)

1 **Coat a 3 1/2- to 4-quart slow cooker with cooking spray.** Place the onions, rice, and water in the slow cooker. Arrange the pork on top, pressing down lightly to allow some of the water to cover the pork.

2 **In a small bowl, combine the bouillon granules, coffee granules, thyme, and black pepper.** Sprinkle evenly over all. Cover and cook on high for 1 1/2 hours, or on low for 3 hours, or until pork is tender.

3 **Turn off the heat.** Using two forks, roughly pull pork apart and stir in the tomatoes, oil, and salt. Sprinkle evenly with the cheese. Cover and let stand 10 minutes to cook the tomatoes slightly and absorb flavors.

Cook's Note:
Adding oil gives the dish a richer texture.

CHAPTER 9
Seafood Entrées

Pico de Gallo Cod with Avocado

Slow Salmon with Horseradish-Dill Sour Cream

Sweet-Home Jumbled Jambalaya

SEAFOOD

Pico de Gallo Cod with Avocado

Makes 4 fillets, 1/2 cup pico de gallo, and 1 cup diced avocado
Serves: 4
Serving Size: 3 ounces cooked fish, 2 tablespoons pico de gallo, and 1/4 cup diced avocado

Exchanges/ Food Choices:
1/2 Carbohydrate
2 Lean Meat
1 Fat

Calories	160
Calories from Fat	60
Total Fat	6g
Saturated Fat	1g
Trans Fat	0g
Monounsaturated Fat	0g
Cholesterol	35mg
Sodium	200mg
Potassium	589mg
Total Carbohydrate	10g
Dietary Fiber	2g
Sugars	4g
Protein	17g

Nonstick cooking spray

1 cup (4 ounces) thinly sliced onion

4 4-ounce fresh or frozen cod fillets, thawed, rinsed, and patted dry

1 teaspoon salt-free steak seasoning blend

1/2 cup freshly prepared pico de gallo

1 ripe medium avocado, peeled, seeded, and diced

1 **Coat a 3 1/2- to 4-quart slow cooker with cooking spray.** Place the onion evenly over the bottom of the slow cooker.

2 **Arrange the fillets in a single layer over the onions.** Sprinkle evenly with the seasoning blend. Cover and cook on high for 1 hour, or on low for 2 hours, or until fillets are opaque in the center.

3 **Remove the fillets and place on serving platter.** Spoon pico de gallo over all and top each with an equal amount of avocado.

Cook's Note:
Fresh pico de gallo is generally a combination of diced tomatoes, jalapeño, onion, cilantro, and lime juice and/or vinegar. It is sold in major supermarkets in the produce or deli section.

Slow Salmon with Horseradish-Dill Sour Cream

Makes 4 fillets and 1/2 cup sour cream mixture
Serves: 4
Serving Size: 3 ounces cooked fillets and 2 tablespoons sour cream mixture

Exchanges/ Food Choices:
1/2 Carbohydrate
4 Lean Meat
1 Fat

Calories	250
Calories from Fat	120
Total Fat	13g
Saturated Fat	2g
Trans Fat	0g
Monounsaturated Fat	6g
Cholesterol	75mg
Sodium	230mg
Potassium	744mg
Total Carbohydrate	7g
Dietary Fiber	1g
Sugars	3g
Protein	27g

SALMON
Nonstick cooking spray

1 medium lemon, cut into 8 slices

4 4-ounce salmon fillets, rinsed and patted dry

1 teaspoon extra-virgin olive oil

1 teaspoon salt-free steak seasoning grilling blend

1/2 teaspoon dried thyme leaves

SOUR CREAM
1/3 cup fat-free sour cream

2 teaspoons prepared horseradish

2 teaspoons minced fresh onion

2 teaspoons fat-free milk

1 tablespoon extra-virgin olive oil

1 teaspoon dried dill weed

1/4 teaspoon salt

1 medium lemon, quartered

1 **Coat a 3 1/2- to 4-quart slow cooker with cooking spray.** Place the lemon slices in the bottom of the slow cooker, overlapping slightly. Arrange the fillets on top of the lemon slices.

2 **Drizzle with 1 teaspoon oil and sprinkle evenly with the steak seasoning blend and the thyme.** Cover and cook on high for 1 hour and 15 minutes, or on low for 2 1/2 hours, or until fish is opaque in center.

3 **In a small bowl whisk together the sour cream ingredients (except lemon wedges).** Cover and refrigerate until time of serving.

4 **Gently remove the salmon from the slow cooker, discarding lemon slices and any pan drippings, and serve with sour cream mixture and lemon wedges.**

Cook's Note:
The lemon slices gently impart a light lemon flavor to the salmon while preventing it from drying out.

SEAFOOD ENTRÉES · SEAFOOD ENT
SEAFOOD ENTRÉES · SEAFOOD ENTRÉES
SEAFOOD ENTRÉES
SEAFOOD ENTRÉES
SEAFOOD
SEAFOOD
SEAFOOD ENTRÉES
SEAFOOD ENTRÉES · SEAFOOD ENTRÉES

Sweet-Home Jumbled Jambalaya

Makes 8 cups shrimp and rice mixture
Serves: 6
Serving Size: 1 1/3 cups

**Exchanges/
Food Choices:**
1 1/2 Carbohydrate
3 Lean Meat
1 Fat

Calories	280
Calories from Fat	110
Total Fat	12g
Saturated Fat	2.5g
Trans Fat	0g
Monounsaturated Fat	3g
Cholesterol	90mg
Sodium	800mg
Potassium	225mg
Total Carbohydrate	21g
Dietary Fiber	3g
Sugars	5g
Protein	23g

Nonstick cooking spray

1 large red bell pepper, cut into 1-inch cubes

1 large yellow bell pepper, cut into 1-inch cubes

1 1/2 cups diced onion

1 medium jalapeño chili pepper, sliced in thin rounds

14.5-ounce can no-salt-added diced tomatoes

1 teaspoon seafood seasoning, such as Old Bay

2 medium dried bay leaves

1/2 teaspoon dried thyme leaves

8 ounces Andouille sausage, thinly sliced

4 medium garlic cloves, minced

1 1/4 cups water

8 ounces raw medium shrimp, peeled

1 cup cooked, diced, chicken breast meat

2 tablespoons extra-virgin olive oil

3/4 cup uncooked instant brown rice

1 **Coat a 3 1/2- to 4-quart slow cooker with cooking spray.** Stir together the bell peppers, onion, jalapeño, tomatoes, seafood seasoning, bay leaves, and thyme in the slow cooker. Cover and cook on high for 3 1/2 hours, or on low for 7 hours, or until onions are tender.

2 **Heat a large skillet coated with cooking spray over medium-high heat.** Brown the sausage 6 minutes, or until richly browned on edges, stirring occasionally. Stir in the garlic and cook 15 seconds, stirring constantly.

3 **Add the water and stir, scraping bottom and sides to release any brown bits.** Add to the slow cooker with the shrimp, chicken, and oil. Cover and cook on high 30 minutes to cook shrimp and allow flavors to absorb.

4 **Cook rice according to package directions, omitting any salt or fat.** Stir into the shrimp mixture. Serve with additional hot sauce, if desired.

Cook's Note:
This is a great way to use up leftover chicken or pork. Add 6 ounces boneless, skinless chicken breast, cut into bite-size pieces, in with the shrimp. May freeze cooled leftovers in 1 1/3-cup portions in airtight containers for up to 1 month.

CHAPTER 10
Meatless Entrées

Mediterranean Eggplant Mounds

Stuffed Peppers with Navy Beans and Pine Nuts

Kalamata White Bean Penne

Wheat Berries, Edamame, and Black Bean Toss

Blue Cheese Portobello Bulgur

Asian Rice with Almonds and Sugar Snap Shreds

Fresh-from-the-Garden Primavera

Pecan-Topped Quinoa Stack Up

Mediterranean Eggplant Mounds

Makes 6 cups
Serves: 4
Serving Size: 1 1/2 cups

**Exchanges/
Food Choices:**
1 Starch
2 Vegetable
2 Lean Meat
1 Fat

Calories	260
Calories from Fat	90
Total Fat	10g
Saturated Fat	3g
Trans Fat	0g
Monounsaturated Fat	3g
Cholesterol	15mg
Sodium	430mg
Potassium	758mg
Total Carbohydrate	26g
Dietary Fiber	7g
Sugars	16g
Protein	17g

MEATLESS

Nonstick cooking spray

2 teaspoons canola oil

8 ounces eggplant, cut into 4 slices, then each slice halved crosswise, creating 8 pieces

1 medium zucchini, thinly sliced

1 1/2 cups diced green bell pepper

2 cups prepared spaghetti sauce

1 cup light cottage cheese

2 egg whites

2 tablespoons dried basil leaves

1/3 cup shredded part-skim mozzarella cheese

2 tablespoons grated Parmesan cheese

1 **Coat a 6-quart slow cooker with cooking spray.**

2 **Heat the oil in a large skillet over medium-high heat.** Tilt the skillet to coat the bottom lightly. Brown the eggplant slices 3 minutes on each side. Remove from heat.

3 **In a medium bowl, stir together the zucchini, bell peppers, and spaghetti sauce.**

4 **In another medium bowl, stir together the cottage cheese, egg whites, and basil.**

5 **Spoon one-third of the vegetable mixture evenly over the bottom of the slow cooker.** Top with four eggplant slices, 1/2 cup cottage cheese mixture, and 2 tablespoons mozzarella cheese.

6 **Repeat the layers: one-third of the vegetable mixture, the remaining 4 eggplant slices, and cottage cheese mixture.** Spoon the remaining vegetable mixture evenly over all.

7 **Cook, covered, on high for 3 hours, or on low for 6 hours, or until vegetables are tender.**

8 **Sprinkle with the remaining mozzarella and Parmesan cheese.** Turn off heat, let stand, uncovered, 15 minutes to allow flavors to blend and absorb some of the liquid.

Stuffed Peppers with Navy Beans and Pine Nuts

Makes 4 peppers and 1 cup sauce

Serves: 4
Serving Size: 1 pepper and 1/4 cup sauce

Exchanges/ Food Choices:

1 1/2 Starch
3 Vegetables
1 Lean Meat
2 Fat

Calories	320
Calories from Fat	100
Total Fat	11g
Saturated Fat	2.5g
Trans Fat	0g
Monounsaturated Fat	4g
Cholesterol	5m
Sodium	530mg
Potassium	555mg
Total Carbohydrate	42g
Dietary Fiber	10g
Sugars	8g
Protein	15g

Nonstick cooking spray

14-ounce can quartered artichoke hearts, drained and coarsely chopped

1/3 cup uncooked instant brown rice

15-ounce can no-salt-added navy beans, rinsed and drained

1/4 cup pine nuts, toasted

1 tablespoon dried oregano leaves

1 tablespoon extra-virgin olive oil

1/2 teaspoon garlic powder

1/4 teaspoon dried pepper flakes, *optional*

4 large green bell peppers

8-ounce can no-salt-added tomato sauce, divided

1/3 cup water

1/4 teaspoon salt

1/4 cup shredded part-skim mozzarella cheese

4 teaspoons grated Parmesan cheese

1 **Coat a 6-quart slow cooker with cooking spray.**

2 **In a medium bowl, stir together the artichokes, rice, beans, pine nuts, oregano, oil, garlic powder, and pepper flakes.**

3 **Cut off the top portion of each bell pepper and remove the seeds and membrane.** Spoon equal amounts of the rice mixture in each of the peppers. Spoon 1 tablespoon tomato sauce on top of each pepper.

4 **Pour the remaining sauce and the water in the bottom of the slow cooker.** Arrange the peppers on the sauce in the slow cooker. Cover and cook on high for 3 hours, or on low for 6 hours, or until peppers are tender.

5 **Place peppers on serving platter.** Stir the salt into the pan drippings and spoon evenly over the peppers, and sprinkle the cheeses evenly over all.

Kalamata White Bean Penne

Makes about 3 cups bean mixture, 2 cups cooked pasta, and 3/4 cup cheese

Serves: 4
Serving Size: 3/4 cup bean mixture, 1/2 cup pasta, and 3 tablespoons cheese

Exchanges/ Food Choices:
2 Starch
1 Vegetable
1 Medium-Fat Meat
1 Fat

Calories	290
Calories from Fat	90
Total Fat	11g
Saturated Fat	3g
Trans Fat	0g
Monounsaturated Fat	4.5g
Cholesterol	5mg
Sodium	500mg
Potassium	415mg
Total Carbohydrate	38g
Dietary Fiber	8g
Sugars	4g
Protein	12g

Nonstick cooking spray

1 medium zucchini, sliced

1 cup grape tomatoes, halved

1 cup diced onion

4 medium garlic cloves, minced

1 1/2 tablespoons dried basil leaves

1/2 teaspoon dried rosemary

1/2 cup dry white wine

1/2 15-ounce can no-salt-added navy beans, rinsed and drained

4 ounces uncooked whole-grain penne pasta

1 cup packed baby spinach

12 pitted kalamata olives, coarsely chopped

1 tablespoon extra-virgin olive oil

3/4 cup crumbled reduced-fat feta cheese

1 **Coat a 3 1/2- to 4-quart slow cooker with cooking spray.** Place the zucchini, tomatoes, onion, garlic, basil, rosemary, and the wine in the slow cooker. Sprinkle the beans over all.

2 **Cover and cook on high for 2 hours, or on low for 4 hours, or until onions are just tender.**

3 **About 20 minutes before serving, prepare the pasta according to package directions, omitting any salt or fats.**

4 **Turn off the slow cooker.** Gently stir in the spinach, olives, and the oil, lightly tossing until the spinach wilts slightly.

5 **Drain the pasta well and place in a pasta bowl or serving platter, top with the bean mixture, and sprinkle the feta evenly over all.**

Wheat Berries, Edamame, and Black Bean Toss

Makes 5 cups
Serves: 6
Serving Size: 3/4 cup

**Exchanges/
Food Choices:**
1 1/2 Starch
1 Lean Meat
1 1/2 Fat

Calories	220
Calories from Fat	100
Total Fat	11g
Saturated Fat	1.5g
Trans Fat	0g
Monounsaturated Fat	4.5g
Cholesterol	5mg
Sodium	530mg
Potassium	345mg
Total Carbohydrate	22g
Dietary Fiber	7g
Sugars	2g
Protein	11g

Nonstick cooking spray

4 cups water

1/2 cup dry wheat berries

1/2 teaspoon dried rosemary

10 ounces shelled edamame

1/2 15-ounce can no-salt-added black beans, rinsed and drained

1 cup grape tomatoes, halved

1/2 cup finely chopped green onion

3 tablespoons canola oil

2 teaspoons grated lemon zest

3/4 teaspoon salt

1/2 cup reduced-fat feta cheese, crumbled (2 ounces)

1 **Coat a 3 1/2- to 4-quart slow cooker with cooking spray.** Stir together the water, wheat berries, and rosemary. Cover and cook on high for 3 hours, or on low for 6 hours, or until softened and chewy.

2 **Turn off the heat.** Stir in the edamame and black beans. Cover and let stand 5 minutes to heat through.

3 **Drain in a fine-mesh strainer, return to the slow cooker, and gently stir in the remaining ingredients, except the cheese.** Sprinkle the cheese on top.

Cook's Note:
A wheat berry is the entire wheat kernel except for the hull (the bran, germ, and endosperm). Wheat berries are sold in health food stores and major supermarkets. Since they take almost an hour to cook on the stove top, they make an ideal slow cooker ingredient.

MEATLESS

Blue Cheese Portobello Bulgur

Makes 4 stuffed mushrooms, 1 cup spinach, and 3 cups cooked bulgur mixture

Serves: 4
Serving Size: 1 stuffed mushroom, 1/4 cup spinach, and 3/4 cup bulgur mixture

Exchanges/ Food Choices:
1/2 Starch
1 Vegetable
1 Medium-Fat Meat
1/2 Fat

Calories	170
Calories from Fat	70
Total Fat	8g
Saturated Fat	3.5g
Trans Fat	0g
Monounsaturated Fat	2.5g
Cholesterol	0mg
Sodium	510mg
Potassium	426mg
Total Carbohydrate	18g
Dietary Fiber	6g
Sugars	3g
Protein	10g

Nonstick cooking spray

1 cup grape tomatoes, quartered

1/2 teaspoon minced fresh garlic

1/2 teaspoon dried rosemary

1/4 teaspoon salt

4 large portobello mushroom caps, wiped clean with damp cloth

1 cup uncooked dry bulgur

6-ounce bag baby spinach

1 tablespoon extra-virgin olive oil

3/4 cup reduced-fat blue cheese (3 ounces)

1 **Coat a 6-quart slow cooker with cooking spray.** In a small bowl, combine the tomatoes, garlic, rosemary, and the salt. Spoon equal amounts on top of the mushrooms.

2 **Place the mushrooms in the slow cooker in a single layer, overlapping slightly if necessary.** Cover and cook on high for 2 hours, or on low for 4 hours, or until mushrooms are tender.

3 **Fifteen minutes before the mushrooms are done, cook the bulgur according to package directions, omitting any salt or fat.** Remove from heat.

4 **Remove the mushrooms with a slotted spoon; set aside.** Cover to keep warm. Stir the spinach and oil into the pan drippings in the slow cooker, cover, and cook on high for 5 minutes.

5 **Using a fork, fluff the bulgur and gently stir in the cheese.** To serve, place equal amounts of the bulgur mixture on each of four dinner plates, top with equal amounts of the spinach mixture, and top with the mushrooms.

Cook's Note:

This makes a "dramatic" presentation. Use 8 smaller mushroom caps instead of the 4 larger Portobello mushrooms and serve as a side dish to 8 people for a variation.

Asian Rice with Almonds and Sugar Snap Shreds

Makes 6 3/4 cups
Serves: 4
Serving Size: 1 2/3 cups

**Exchanges/
Food Choices:**
1 1/2 Starch
1 Vegetable
1 Lean Meat
2 Fat

Calories	270
Calories from Fat	110
Total Fat	13g
Saturated Fat	1g
Trans Fat	0g
Monounsaturated Fat	6.5g
Cholesterol	0mg
Sodium	300mg
Potassium	305mg
Total Carbohydrate	31g
Dietary Fiber	6g
Sugars	5g
Protein	9g

Nonstick cooking spray

2 cups water

1 1/2 cups diced onion

1 cup uncooked brown rice, preferably parboiled variety

1/8 teaspoon dried pepper flakes

1 cup fresh sugar snap peas, cut in thirds lengthwise

3/4 cup shelled fresh or frozen edamame

2 ounces (1/2 cup) slivered almonds, toasted

1 tablespoon canola oil

2 medium garlic cloves, minced

1/2 cup chopped fresh cilantro leaves

2 tablespoons chopped fresh basil leaves

1 teaspoon grated gingerroot

1/2 teaspoon salt

1. **Coat a 3 1/2- to 4-quart slow cooker with cooking spray.** Place the water, onion, rice, and pepper flakes in the slow cooker. Cover and cook on high for 1 1/2 hours or on low for 3 hours.

2. **Turn off the heat.** Fluff the rice with a fork. Stir in the sugar snaps, edamame, almonds, oil, and garlic. Cover and let stand 10 minutes. Stir in the remaining ingredients.

Cook's Note:
Substitute the edamame with 3/4 cup cooked diced chicken breast meat or cooked shrimp, if desired.

Fresh-from-the-Garden Primavera

Makes 4 cups
Serves: 4
Serving Size: 1 cup pasta mixture plus 1 tablespoon cheese

**Exchanges/
Food Choices:**
1 1/2 Starch
1 Vegetable
2 1/2 Fat

Calories	280
Calories from Fat	130
Total Fat	14g
Saturated Fat	2.5g
Trans Fat	0g
Monounsaturated Fat	5.5g
Cholesterol	5mg
Sodium	490mg
Potassium	501mg
Total Carbohydrate	28g
Dietary Fiber	6g
Sugars	3g
Protein	10g

Nonstick cooking spray

1 medium yellow squash, cut in half lengthwise and sliced

1 cup grape tomatoes, halved

2 medium jalapeños, finely chopped

2 tablespoons water

2 cups small broccoli florets

4 ounces uncooked whole-grain spaghetti noodles, broken into thirds

2 tablespoons canola oil

1/4 cup finely chopped fresh parsley

1/4 cup pine nuts, toasted

1/2 teaspoon salt

1/4 cup grated Parmesan cheese

1 **Coat a 3 1/2- to 4-quart slow cooker with cooking spray.** Place the squash, tomatoes, jalapeños, and the water in the slow cooker. Cover and cook on low only for 2 hours or until the vegetables are tender.

2 **Fifteen minutes before the vegetables are done, add the broccoli to the slow cooker.**

3 **In a large saucepan, cook the pasta according to package directions, omitting any salt or fats.** Drain pasta and add to the vegetables in the slow cooker with the remaining ingredients, except the cheese. Serve topped with cheese.

Pecan-Topped Quinoa Stack Up

Makes 6 cups
Serves: 4
Serving Size: 1 1/2 cups

**Exchanges/
Food Choices:**
2 Starch
1/2 Fruit
1 Vegetable
3 1/2 Fat

Calories	370
Calories from Fat	150
Total Fat	17g
Saturated Fat	1.5g
Trans Fat	0g
Monounsaturated Fat	9g
Cholesterol	0mg
Sodium	440mg
Potassium	501mg
Total Carbohydrate	48g
Dietary Fiber	8g
Sugars	14g
Protein	10g

Nonstick cooking spray

1 cup uncooked dry quinoa

1 cup thinly sliced carrots

2 1/2 cups water

1/2 8-ounce can sliced water chestnuts, cut in half

2 tablespoons light soy sauce

1 tablespoon balsamic vinegar

1 tablespoon canola oil

1/4 teaspoon salt

1/2 cup frozen green peas, thawed

1/4 cup golden raisins or chopped dried apricots

2 ounces (1/2 cup) pecan pieces, toasted

1 **Coat a 3 1/2- to 4-quart slow cooker with cooking spray.** Stir together the quinoa, carrots, and water in the slow cooker. Cover and cook on high for 1 hour, or on low for 2 hours, or until water is absorbed.

2 **Turn off the heat.** Stir in the water chestnuts.

3 **In a small bowl, stir together the soy sauce, vinegar, oil, and salt.** Place the quinoa mixture on a serving platter. Sprinkle with the peas and raisins. Spoon the soy sauce mixture evenly over all and sprinkle with the pecans.

CHAPTER 11

Side Dishes

Artichokes with Buttery Lemon Sauce

Red Cabbage, Red Apple Braise

Vanilla-Pecan Carrots

New and Natural Country Collards

Buttery Black Pepper-Parsley Cob Corn

Smoky, Creamy Chili Pepper Corn

Creamy White Grits

Roasted Parmesan New Potatoes

So-Easy Sour Cream Mashed Potatoes

Golden Potatoes with Blue Cheese

Hometown Hash Brown Casserole

Yukon Gold Potatoes and Fennel

"Baked" Sweet Potatoes with Buttery Honey

Sweet Potato-Parsnip Casserole

Lemon-Parsley Bright Rice

Orange-Zested Wild Rice

Curried Apple-Raisin Acorn Squash

Cheddary Yellow Squash Casserole

Zucchini, Corn, and Grape Tomato Bowl

Slow "Baked" Tomatoes with Olives

Cornbread Loaf

Chunky Cherry-Peach Preserves

Baked Pear-Apricot Fruit Spread

SIDES

Artichokes with Buttery Lemon Sauce

**Makes 4 artichokes and
1/4 cup sauce**
Serves: 4
Serving Size: 1 artichoke
and 1 tablespoon sauce

**Exchanges/
Food Choices:**
2 Vegetable
1 1/2 Fat

Calories	120
Calories from Fat	50
Total Fat	6g
Saturated Fat	1.5g
Trans Fat	0g
Monounsaturated Fat	2g
Cholesterol	0mg
Sodium	380mg
Potassium	400mg
Total Carbohydrate	18g
Dietary Fiber	12g
Sugars	2g
Protein	4g

ARTICHOKES
4 medium globe
   artichokes, rinsed

2 cups hot water

2 medium lemons, halved
   crosswise

1/4 teaspoon salt

SAUCE
1/4 cup trans-fat-free
   margarine

1 tablespoon finely
   chopped fresh parsley

1/4 teaspoon grated
   lemon zest, *optional*

1/2 medium lemon

1/8 teaspoon salt

1   **Cut off stems of artichokes, and
    remove bottom leaves.** Trim about a
    1/2 inch from tops of artichokes.

2   **Place the water in a 6-quart slow
    cooker.** Place the artichokes, stem
    side down, in the slow cooker.
    Squeeze the juice of two lemons
    evenly over all and sprinkle with
    1/4 teaspoon salt. Cover and cook
    on low for 6–7 hours or until a leaf
    near the center of each artichoke
    pulls out easily.

3   **Place the margarine in a
    microwave-safe small bowl.** Cook
    on high for 25–30 seconds or until
    slightly melted. Stir in the parsley
    and the lemon zest, if desired.

4   **Remove artichokes from slow
    cooker and place on a serving plate
    or a rimmed platter.** Squeeze the
    juice of the remaining lemon half
    over all and spoon the margarine
    over each artichoke. Sprinkle lightly
    with the remaining
    1/8 teaspoon salt.

Red Cabbage, Red Apple Braise

SI
SIDE DISHES
SIDE DISHES
SIDE DISHES
SIDE DISHES
SIDE DISHES
SIDE DISHES

SIDE DISHES

Makes 4 cups
Serves: 8
Serving Size: 1/2 cup

**Exchanges/
Food Choices:**
1/2 Fruit
1 Vegetable

Calories	70
Calories from Fat	10
Total Fat	1g
Saturated Fat	0g
Trans Fat	0g
Monounsaturated Fat	0g
Cholesterol	5mg
Sodium	280mg
Potassium	198mg
Total Carbohydrate	13g
Dietary Fiber	4g
Sugars	8g
Protein	3g

Nonstick cooking spray

9 cups (about 1 pound) coarsely shredded red cabbage

2 medium apples, halved, cored, and chopped

1 medium onion (4 ounces), thinly sliced

1/4 cup red wine vinegar

1/2 teaspoon ground allspice

1/8 teaspoon dried pepper flakes, *optional*

1/4 cup natural bacon bits

1/2 teaspoon salt

1 **Coat a 3 1/2- to 4-quart slow cooker with cooking spray.** Stir together all the ingredients, except the bacon and salt, in the slow cooker. Cover and cook on high for 1 hour and 45 minutes, or on low for 3 1/2 hours, or until vegetables are tender crisp.

2 **Turn off the heat.** Stir in the bacon and salt. Let stand, uncovered, 15 minutes to absorb flavors. Remove with a slotted spoon and place in a serving bowl.

3 **Serve warm or chilled.**

Cook's Note:
This is delicious served with roast pork or chicken. Serve it as a side dish or a wilted salad.

Vanilla-Pecan Carrots

Makes 3 cups
Serves: 6
Serving Size: 1/2 cup

**Exchanges/
Food Choices:**
2 Vegetable
1 Fat

Calories	100
Calories from Fat	50
Total Fat	5g
Saturated Fat	0.5g
Trans Fat	0g
Monounsaturated Fat	3g
Cholesterol	0mg
Sodium	95mg
Potassium	253mg
Total Carbohydrate	9g
Dietary Fiber	3g
Sugars	5g
Protein	1g

Nonstick cooking spray

3 cups sliced carrots

1 medium onion (4 ounces), cut into 8 wedges

1/4 cup pecan pieces

2 teaspoons canola oil

2 tablespoons packed brown sugar substitute blend, such as Splenda

1 teaspoon trans-fat-free margarine

1/2 teaspoon apple or pumpkin pie spice **or** 1/4 teaspoon ground cinnamon

1/4 teaspoon ground nutmeg

1/2 teaspoon vanilla, butter, and nut flavoring **or** 3/4 teaspoon vanilla extract

1/8 teaspoon salt

1 **Coat a 3 1/2- to 4-quart slow cooker with cooking spray.** Place the carrots, onion, and pecans in the slow cooker.

2 **Drizzle oil evenly over all and toss to coat.** Cover and cook on high for 3 hours, or on low for 6 hours, or until tender.

3 **Stir in the remaining ingredients and toss until well blended.**

New and Natural Country Collards

Makes 4 cups
Serves: 8
Serving Size: 1/2 cup

**Exchanges/
Food Choices:**
1 Vegetable
1/2 Fat

Calories	35
Calories from Fat	20
Total Fat	2g
Saturated Fat	0g
Trans Fat	0g
Monounsaturated Fat	1g
Cholesterol	0mg
Sodium	230mg
Potassium	99mg
Total Carbohydrate	4g
Dietary Fiber	2g
Sugars	1g
Protein	1g

Nonstick cooking spray

16-ounce bag fresh
collard greens

2 1/2 quarts hot water

1 1/2 teaspoons sugar

1 teaspoon dried thyme
leaves

1/2 teaspoon garlic
powder

1 tablespoon canola oil

3/4 teaspoon salt

1 **Coat a 6-quart slow cooker
with cooking spray.** Place all the
ingredients, except the oil and salt,
in the slow cooker. Cover and cook
on high for 4 hours, or on low for
8 hours, or until just tender.

2 **Drain collards, reserving 1/3 cup
liquid.** Return the collards and the
reserved liquid to the slow cooker.
Stir in the oil and salt. Cover and
cook 15 minutes on high to allow
flavors to absorb.

Buttery Black Pepper-Parsley Cob Corn

Makes 4 medium ears of corn and about 1/4 cup parsley mixture
Serves: 4
Serving Size: 1 ear of corn and about 1 tablespoon parsley mixture

Exchanges/ Food Choices:
1 Starch
1 Fat

Calories	120
Calories from Fat	50
Total Fat	5g
Saturated Fat	0.5g
Trans Fat	0g
Monounsaturated Fat	1g
Cholesterol	0mg
Sodium	190mg
Potassium	265mg
Total Carbohydrate	18g
Dietary Fiber	2g
Sugars	5g
Protein	4g

4 medium ears of corn, husks and silk removed

2 tablespoons trans-fat-free margarine, softened

2 tablespoons finely chopped fresh parsley

1/2 teaspoon salt-free steak seasoning blend

1/4 teaspoon paprika

1/4 teaspoon salt

1   **Wrap each ear of corn in a sheet of foil.** Place in a 3 1/2- to 4-quart slow cooker. Cover and cook on high for 2 1/2–3 hours or until tender.

2   **In a small bowl, stir together the remaining ingredients.** Cover and refrigerate until time of serving.

3   **Remove the foil from each ear of corn;** spread equal amounts of the margarine mixture on each.

Smoky, Creamy Chili Pepper Corn

Makes 3 cups
Serves: 6
Serving Size: 1/2 cup

**Exchanges/
Food Choices:**
1 Starch
1 Vegetable
1/2 Fat

Calories	130
Calories from Fat	25
Total Fat	3g
Saturated Fat	1.5g
Trans Fat	0g
Monounsaturated Fat	0.5g
Cholesterol	10mg
Sodium	260mg
Potassium	306mg
Total Carbohydrate	23g
Dietary Fiber	3g
Sugars	4g
Protein	4g

Nonstick cooking spray

1 pound frozen corn kernels, thawed

2 medium poblano chili peppers, seeded and diced

1 cup diced red bell pepper

1/2 cup diced onion

1–1 1/2 teaspoons smoked paprika

1/2 teaspoon black pepper

1/4 cup fat-free half-and-half

3 ounces light cream cheese, cut in small pieces

1/4 teaspoon salt

1 **Coat a 3 1/2- to 4-quart slow cooker with cooking spray.** Place the corn, chili peppers, bell peppers, onion, paprika, and black pepper in the slow cooker. Cover and cook on high for 3 hours, or on low for 5 1/2–6 hours, or until onions are tender.

2 **Stir in the remaining ingredients, cover, and cook 15 minutes or until cream cheese has melted.**

Creamy White Grits

Makes 4 cups
Serves: 8
Serving Size: 1/2 cup

**Exchanges/
Food Choices:**
1 Starch
1/2 Fat

Calories	110
Calories from Fat	20
Total Fat	2g
Saturated Fat	1.5g
Trans Fat	0g
Monounsaturated Fat	0.5g
Cholesterol	10mg
Sodium	360mg
Potassium	66mg
Total Carbohydrate	18g
Dietary Fiber	1g
Sugars	1g
Protein	3g

Nonstick cooking spray

4 cups water

1 cup dry white corn grits, old-fashioned variety

1/2 teaspoon garlic powder

1/4 cup fat-free milk

4 ounces light cream cheese

1 teaspoon salt

1 **Coat a 3 1/2- to 4-quart slow cooker with cooking spray.** Stir together water, grits, and garlic powder in the slow cooker.

2 **Cover and cook on high for 1 1/2 hours stirring every 30 minutes, or on low for 3 hours stirring every hour, or until grits are creamy and tender.**

3 **Stir in the remaining ingredients.** Turn off the heat and let stand, covered, 10 minutes to absorb flavors and thicken slightly.

Cook's Note:
Stirring the grits occasionally helps the grits cook evenly and not form lumps. For a thinner consistency, add additional milk.

Roasted Parmesan New Potatoes

Makes 16 potato halves
Serves: 4
Serving Size: 4 potato halves

**Exchanges/
Food Choices:**
1 Starch
1/2 Fat

Calories	120
Calories from Fat	30
Total Fat	3.5g
Saturated Fat	1g
Trans Fat	0g
Monounsaturated Fat	1.5g
Cholesterol	5mg
Sodium	210mg
Potassium	492mg
Total Carbohydrate	20g
Dietary Fiber	2g
Sugars	1g
Protein	4g

Nonstick cooking spray

8 new potatoes (1 pound total), halved

2 teaspoons extra-virgin olive oil

1 teaspoon dried oregano leaves

1/2 teaspoon dried rosemary

1/4 teaspoon paprika

1/4 teaspoon crushed red pepper flakes

2 tablespoons water

1/4 teaspoon salt

2 tablespoons grated Parmesan cheese

2 tablespoons chopped fresh parsley

1 **Coat a 3 1/2- to 4-quart slow cooker with cooking spray.** Place the potatoes in the slow cooker, drizzle with the oil, and toss until well coated.

2 **Stir in the oregano, rosemary, paprika, and the pepper flakes.** Cover and cook on high for 3 hours, or on low for 5 1/2–6 hours, or until tender.

3 **Turn off the heat.** Add the water and salt to the potatoes in the slow cooker and stir, scraping up any browned bits with a rubber spatula. Sprinkle the Parmesan and parsley over all. Let stand, uncovered, 10 minutes to absorb flavors.

So-Easy Sour Cream Mashed Potatoes

Makes 4 cups
Serves: 8
Serving Size: 1/2 cup

**Exchanges/
Food Choices:**
1 1/2 Starch
1/2 Fat

Calories	130
Calories from Fat	35
Total Fat	4g
Saturated Fat	1g
Trans Fat	0g
Monounsaturated Fat	1g
Cholesterol	0mg
Sodium	290mg
Potassium	521mg
Total Carbohydrate	22g
Dietary Fiber	2g
Sugars	2g
Protein	3g

Nonstick cooking spray

2 pounds baking potatoes, diced

1 cup water

1/2 cup fat-free milk

1/3 cup trans-fat-free margarine

1/4 cup fat-free sour cream

3/4 teaspoon salt

1/2 teaspoon black pepper

1/4 teaspoon dried thyme leaves

1/4 teaspoon garlic powder

1   **Coat a 3 1/2- to 4-quart slow cooker with cooking spray.** Place the potatoes and water in slow cooker. Cook on high for 3 hours, or low for 5 1/2–6 hours, or until tender.

2   **Add the remaining ingredients and mash, using a potato masher or hand-held electric mixer, to desired consistency.**

Golden Potatoes with Blue Cheese

Makes 4 cups
Serves: 8
Serving Size: 1/2 cup

**Exchanges/
Food Choices:**
1 Starch
1 Fat

Calories	120
Calories from Fat	35
Total Fat	4g
Saturated Fat	1.5g
Trans Fat	0g
Monounsaturated Fat	1.5g
Cholesterol	0mg
Sodium	250mg
Potassium	37mg
Total Carbohydrate	17g
Dietary Fiber	1g
Sugars	1g
Protein	4g

Nonstick cooking spray

1/2 teaspoon dried
oregano leaves

1/2 teaspoon garlic
powder

1/2 teaspoon salt

1 1/2 pounds Yukon gold
potatoes, thinly sliced

1 cup diced onion

2 ounces (1/2 cup)
reduced-fat blue cheese,
crumbled, divided

1 1/2 tablespoons extra-
virgin olive oil

2 tablespoons finely
chopped fresh parsley

1 **Coat a 5- to 6-quart slow cooker
with cooking spray.**

2 **In a small bowl, combine the
oregano, garlic powder, and salt.**
Arrange half of the potatoes in the
bottom of the slow cooker; sprinkle
evenly with the onions.

3 **Sprinkle half of the oregano
mixture and half of the cheese
evenly over all.** Repeat with the
remaining potatoes and oregano
mixture. Drizzle the oil over all.

4 **Cover and cook on high for
3 1/2–4 hours, or on low for
6 1/2–7 hours, or until potatoes
are tender.** Sprinkle with the
remaining cheese and parsley. Let
stand, uncovered, 15 minutes to
absorb liquid and allow cheese to
melt slightly.

Cook's Note:
You can halve the recipe and cook
in a 3 1/2- to 4-quart slow cooker,
if desired.

SIDE DISHES SIDE DISHES SIDE DISHES SIDE DISHES SIDE DISHES SIDE DISHES SIDE DISHES SIDE DISHES SIDE DISHES ES SIDE DISHES

SIDES

SIDE DISHES SIDE DISHES SIDE DISHES SIDE DISHES SIDE DISHES SIDE DISHES SI

Hometown Hash Brown Casserole

Makes 4 cups
Serves: 8
Serving Size: 1/2 cup

**Exchanges/
Food Choices:**
1/2 Starch
1 Vegetable
1 Fat

Calories	110
Calories from Fat	50
Total Fat	5g
Saturated Fat	1.5g
Trans Fat	0g
Monounsaturated Fat	2.5g
Cholesterol	5mg
Sodium	290mg
Potassium	271mg
Total Carbohydrate	14g
Dietary Fiber	2g
Sugars	2g
Protein	3g

Nonstick cooking spray

1 pound frozen hash browns, cubed variety

1 1/2 cups diced onion

1 1/2 cups diced green bell pepper

1/2 teaspoon dried oregano leaves

1/2 teaspoon black pepper

1/4 cup light cream cheese

2 tablespoons canola oil

3/4 teaspoon salt, divided

1 ounce (1/4 cup) reduced-fat sharp Cheddar cheese, shredded

1 **Coat a 3 1/2- to 4-quart slow cooker with cooking spray.** Stir together all ingredients, except 1/4 teaspoon salt and the cheese, in the slow cooker.

2 **Cover and cook on high for 2 1/2 hours, or on low for 4 1/2 hours, or until potatoes and onions are tender.**

3 **Turn off the heat.** Sprinkle with remaining salt and cheese. Let stand, uncovered, for 25 minutes to absorb liquid and achieve proper texture.

Yukon Gold Potatoes and Fennel

Makes 5 cups
Serves: 10
Serving Size: 1/2 cup

**Exchanges/
Food Choices:**
1/2 Starch
1 Vegetable
1/2 Fat

Calories	90
Calories from Fat	35
Total Fat	4.5g
Saturated Fat	0.5g
Trans Fat	0g
Monounsaturated Fat	3g
Cholesterol	0mg
Sodium	200mg
Potassium	152mg
Total Carbohydrate	13g
Dietary Fiber	2g
Sugars	2g
Protein	2g

Nonstick cooking spray

1 pound Yukon gold potatoes, cut into 1-inch cubes

4 medium carrots, cut into 1-inch pieces

1 1/2 cups sliced fennel bulb, cut into 1/8-inch-thick slices

1 medium onion (4 ounces), cut into 1/2-inch wedges

1 teaspoon dried thyme leaves

1/4 teaspoon ground nutmeg

3 tablespoons extra-virgin olive oil

3/4 teaspoon salt

1 **Coat a 3 1/2- to 4-quart slow cooker with cooking spray.** Stir together all the ingredients, except the salt, in the slow cooker. Cover and cook on high for 3 1/2 hours, or on low for 7 hours, or until vegetables are tender.

2 **Gently, stir in the salt.** Turn off the heat. Let stand, uncovered, 15 minutes to absorb flavors.

Cook's Note:
This would be perfect for a potluck or family gathering.

"Baked" Sweet Potatoes with Buttery Honey

**Makes 2 potatoes and
8 teaspoons honey
mixture**
Serves: 4
Serving Size: 1/2 potato and
about 2 teaspoons honey
mixture

**Exchanges/
Food Choices:**
1 Starch
1/2 Fat

Calories	90
Calories from Fat	25
Total Fat	3g
Saturated Fat	0.5g
Trans Fat	0g
Monounsaturated Fat	1g
Cholesterol	0mg
Sodium	135mg
Potassium	277mg
Total Carbohydrate	16g
Dietary Fiber	2g
Sugars	8g
Protein	1g

Nonstick cooking spray

2 8-ounce sweet potatoes,
pierced in several areas
with a fork

2 tablespoons trans-fat-
free margarine

1 tablespoon honey

1/2 teaspoon vanilla

1/4 teaspoon ground
nutmeg

1/8 teaspoon salt

1 **Lightly coat a 3 1/2- to 4-quart
slow cooker with cooking spray.**
Wrap each potato in foil and place
in the slow cooker. Cover and cook
on high for 3 hours, or on low for
6 hours, or until potatoes are tender
when pierced with a fork.

2 **Meanwhile, stir together the
remaining ingredients in a small
bowl.** Refrigerate until time of
serving.

3 **Split potatoes in half lengthwise,
fluff with a fork, and top each half
with an equal amount of the honey
mixture.**

Cook's Note:
This may be doubled to serve 8, if
desired, using the same times and
temperatures.

Sweet Potato-Parsnip Casserole

Makes 4 cups
Serves: 8
Serving Size: 1/2 cup

**Exchanges/
Food Choices:**
1 Starch
1 Vegetable
1/2 Fat

Calories	120
Calories from Fat	30
Total Fat	3.5g
Saturated Fat	0g
Trans Fat	0g
Monounsaturated Fat	2g
Cholesterol	0mg
Sodium	190mg
Potassium	341mg
Total Carbohydrate	21g
Dietary Fiber	3g
Sugars	6g
Protein	2g

Nonstick cooking spray

1 1/2 pounds sweet potatoes, peeled and cut into 3/4-inch cubes

1 medium parsnip, peeled and diced

1/2 cup diced onion

2 tablespoons canola oil

2 teaspoons sugar

1/2 teaspoon dried thyme leaves

1/8 teaspoon ground nutmeg

1/2 teaspoon salt

1/4 teaspoon black pepper

1 **Coat a 3 1/2- to 4-quart slow cooker with cooking spray.** Stir together all the ingredients in the slow cooker. Cover and cook on high for 3 hours and 15 minutes, or on low for 6 1/2 hours, or until potatoes are very tender.

2 **Turn off the heat.** Let stand, uncovered, 15 minutes to absorb liquid and achieve proper texture.

Cook's Note:
Be sure to cut the vegetables to the sizes given in the ingredient list for even cooking and peak flavors.

Lemon-Parsley Bright Rice

Makes 4 cups
Serves: 8
Serving Size: 1/2 cup

**Exchanges/
Food Choices:**
1 Starch
1 Fat

Calories	120
Calories from Fat	40
Total Fat	4.5g
Saturated Fat	0.5g
Trans Fat	0g
Monounsaturated Fat	2g
Cholesterol	0mg
Sodium	330mg
Potassium	27mg
Total Carbohydrate	19g
Dietary Fiber	1g
Sugars	6g
Protein	1g

Nonstick cooking spray

1 cup uncooked brown rice, preferably parboiled variety

1 cup diced yellow bell pepper

2 cups water

1/2 teaspoon ground turmeric

3 tablespoons trans-fat-free margarine

1 tablespoon extra-virgin olive oil

2–3 teaspoons grated lemon zest

1/2 teaspoon salt

1/2 cup chopped fresh parsley

1 **Coat a 3 1/2- to 4-quart slow cooker with cooking spray.** Stir together the rice, bell pepper, water, and turmeric in the slow cooker. Cover and cook on high for 1 1/2 hours or on low for 3 hours.

2 **Fluff rice mixture with a fork and stir in the remaining ingredients, except the parsley.** Sprinkle with the parsley.

SIDE DISHES SIDE DISHES SIDE DISHES SIDE DISHES SIDE DISHES SIDE DISHES SIDE DISHES SIDE DISHES SIDE DISHES SIDE DISHES SIDE DISHES SIDE DISHES SIDE DISHES SIDE DISHES

SIDES

Orange-Zested Wild Rice

Makes 4 cups
Serves: 8
Serving Size: 1/2 cup

**Exchanges/
Food Choices:**
1 1/2 Carbohydrate
1 Fat

Calories	150
Calories from Fat	60
Total Fat	6g
Saturated Fat	0.5g
Trans Fat	0g
Monounsaturated Fat	1g
Cholesterol	0mg
Sodium	210mg
Potassium	122mg
Total Carbohydrate	22g
Dietary Fiber	4g
Sugars	7g
Protein	4g

Nonstick cooking spray

2 teaspoons sesame oil, divided

1 cup diced onion

1 cup diced green or red bell pepper

1/2 cup diced carrots

1/3 cup dried cranberries

3 ounces uncooked wild rice

1/8 teaspoon dried pepper flakes

1 3/4 cups hot water

8-ounce can sliced water chestnuts, drained and cut in thin strips

1/2 cup chopped walnuts

2 tablespoons light soy sauce

1 1/2 teaspoons sugar

1 1/2 teaspoons grated orange zest

1/4 teaspoon salt

1 **Coat a 3 1/2- to 4-quart slow cooker with cooking spray.**

2 **Heat 1 teaspoon oil in a medium nonstick skillet over medium-high heat.** Tilt the skillet to lightly coat bottom. Cook the onions 6 minutes or until richly browned, stirring frequently.

3 **Add the onions, bell pepper, carrots, cranberries, wild rice, pepper flakes, and water to the slow cooker.** Stir to blend. Cover and cook on high for 2 1/2 hours, or on low for 4 1/2–5 hours, or until rice is cooked.

4 **Stir in the remaining ingredients.**

Cook's Note:
Be sure to use hot water or the rice will not cook properly.

Curried Apple-Raisin Acorn Squash

Makes 4 squash wedges and about 1 1/3 cups apple mixture
Serves: 4
Serving Size: 1 squash wedge and about 1/3 cup apple mixture

Exchanges/
Food Choices:
1 Starch
1 Fruit
1 Fat

Calories	190
Calories from Fat	60
Total Fat	7g
Saturated Fat	1g
Trans Fat	0g
Monounsaturated Fat	3g
Cholesterol	0mg
Sodium	100mg
Potassium	557mg
Total Carbohydrate	33g
Dietary Fiber	4g
Sugars	18g
Protein	2g

Nonstick cooking spray

2 cups diced apples, such as Granny Smith

1/4 cup raisins

1/4 cup pecan pieces

1/4 cup water

1 teaspoon curry powder

1/2 teaspoon ground cinnamon

1/8 teaspoon salt

1 large acorn squash (about 1 1/2 pounds total), cut into 4 wedges with stems and strings discarded

1 tablespoon trans-fat-free margarine

2 teaspoons vanilla extract

1 tablespoon honey

1 **Coat a 3 1/2- to 4-quart slow cooker with cooking spray.** Place the apples, raisins, pecans, water, curry powder, cinnamon, and salt in the bottom of the slow cooker. Stir until well blended.

2 **Place the squash wedges on top of the apple mixture, making sure that an edge of each squash wedge touches the apple mixture.** Cover and cook on high for 2 hours, or on low for 4 hours, or until the squash is tender when pierced with a fork.

3 **Place the squash wedges on a serving plate; stir together the apple mixture with the margarine.** Spoon equal amounts of the apple mixture on top of the squash wedges and drizzle honey over all.

Cook's Note:
To make squash easier to cut, pierce the outer skin in several areas with a fork. Place the squash on a paper towel in the microwave and cook on high for 2–2 1/2 minutes, no longer. Place on a cutting board and use a clean dish towel to hold the squash in place while cutting.

Cheddary Yellow Squash Casserole

Makes 3 cups
Serves: 6
Serving Size: 1/2 cup

**Exchanges/
Food Choices:**
2 Vegetable
1/2 Fat

Calories	70
Calories from Fat	20
Total Fat	2.5g
Saturated Fat	1.5g
Trans Fat	0g
Monounsaturated Fat	0g
Cholesterol	5mg
Sodium	310mg
Potassium	293mg
Total Carbohydrate	9g
Dietary Fiber	3g
Sugars	4g
Protein	4g

Nonstick cooking spray

1 pound yellow crookneck squash, sliced

1 cup diced onion

1/2 cup matchstick carrots

1/2 cup diced red or green bell pepper

1/2 teaspoon dried thyme leaves

1/4 teaspoon black pepper

1 slice low-calorie whole-wheat bread, torn in smaller pieces

1/2 teaspoon salt

1/2 cup shredded reduced-fat sharp Cheddar cheese

1 **Coat a 3 1/2- to 4-quart slow cooker with cooking spray.** Place the squash, onions, carrots, bell peppers, thyme, and black pepper in the slow cooker. Cover and cook on high for 2 hours, or on low for 3 1/2–4 hours, or until squash is tender.

2 **Place the bread pieces in a blender or food processor.** Secure with lid and pulse to a coarse crumb texture.

3 **Heat a medium nonstick skillet over medium-high heat.** Brown the bread crumbs for 2 minutes, stirring constantly. Immediately remove from skillet and set aside on separate plate.

4 **When squash is done, turn off the heat and gently stir in the salt.** Sprinkle with the cheese and top with the bread crumbs. Let stand 15 minutes, uncovered, to absorb the liquid.

SIDE DISHES · SIDE DISHES · SIDE DISHES · SIDE DISHES · SIDE DISHES · SIDE DISHES · SIDE DISHES · SIDE DISHES · SIDE DISHES · SIDE DISHES

SIDES

SIDE DISHES   SIDE DISHES   SIDE DISHES   SIDE DISHES   SIDE DISHES   SIDE DISHES   SIDE DISHES   SIDE DISHES   SIDE DISHES   SIDE DISHES   SIDE DISHES   SIDE DISHES   S

SIDES

Zucchini, Corn, and Grape Tomato Bowl

Makes 4 cups
Serves: 8
Serving Size: 1/2 cup

**Exchanges/
Food Choices:**
1/2 Starch
1 Vegetable

Calories	60
Calories from Fat	20
Total Fat	2g
Saturated Fat	0g
Trans Fat	0g
Monounsaturated Fat	1g
Cholesterol	0mg
Sodium	230mg
Potassium	210mg
Total Carbohydrate	11g
Dietary Fiber	2g
Sugars	3g
Protein	2g

Nonstick cooking spray

2 medium zucchini,
   quartered lengthwise
   and cut into 1-inch
   pieces

1 medium onion
   (4 ounces), cut into
   8 wedges

2 cups frozen corn

1 jalapeño pepper, seeded,
   if desired, and finely
   chopped

2 medium garlic cloves,
   minced

1 tablespoon extra-virgin
   olive oil

2 cups (1 pint) grape
   tomatoes, halved

1/4 cup chopped fresh
   parsley

3/4 teaspoon salt

1 **Coat a 3 1/2- to 4-quart slow
   cooker with cooking spray.** Stir
   together zucchini, onion, corn,
   jalapeño, garlic, and oil in the slow
   cooker.

2 **Cover and cook on high for 1 hour
   and 15 minutes, or on low for
   2 1/2 hours, or until vegetables are
   tender crisp.** Stir in the tomatoes.
   Cover and cook 10 minutes
   until heated. Stir in remaining
   ingredients.

Cook's Note:
This is the perfect dish to free
up your stovetop and minimize
monitoring when you're expecting a
crowd.

Slow "Baked" Tomatoes with Olives

Makes 4 tomato halves
Serves: 4
Serving Size: 1 tomato half

**Exchanges/
Food Choices:**
1 Vegetable
1 Fat

Calories	80
Calories from Fat	45
Total Fat	5g
Saturated Fat	0.5g
Trans Fat	0g
Monounsaturated Fat	2.5g
Cholesterol	0mg
Sodium	280mg
Potassium	226mg
Total Carbohydrate	5g
Dietary Fiber	2g
Sugars	3g
Protein	3g

Nonstick cooking spray

2 large tomatoes (about 8 ounces each), halved crosswise

1/2 4-ounce can chopped ripe olives

1 1/2 teaspoons dried basil leaves

2 teaspoons balsamic vinegar

2 teaspoons extra-virgin olive oil

1/8 teaspoon salt

1/4 cup crumbled reduced-fat blue cheese

1 **Coat a 3 1/2- to 4-quart slow cooker with cooking spray.** Place tomatoes in bottom of slow cooker, cut side up. In a small bowl, combine the olives, basil, vinegar, and oil. Spoon equal amounts over each tomato half.

2 **Cover and cook on high for 1 hour, or on low for 2 hours, or until tomatoes are just tender.** Carefully remove the tomato halves and spoon pan drippings evenly over the tomatoes. Let stand 5 minutes to absorb flavors and sprinkle evenly with the salt and cheese.

Cook's Note:

To remove the tomatoes easily, use 2 tablespoons, one on each side of each tomato, and lift straight up to serving platter.

Cornbread Loaf

Makes 1 loaf
Serves: 12
Serving Size: 3/4-inch slice

**Exchanges/
Food Choices:**
1 1/2 Starch
1/2 Fat

Calories	130
Calories from Fat	30
Total Fat	3g
Saturated Fat	0g
Trans Fat	0g
Monounsaturated	1.5g
Cholesterol	0mg
Sodium	230mg
Potassium	71mg
Total Carbohydrate	22g
Dietary Fiber	1g
Sugars	3g
Protein	4g

Nonstick cooking spray

1 cup all-purpose flour

1 cup yellow plain cornmeal

1 1/2 tablespoons sugar

1 tablespoon baking powder

1/4 teaspoon salt

1/8 teaspoon cayenne pepper

1 1/4 cups 1%-fat buttermilk

1/4 cup egg substitute

2 tablespoons canola oil

1/4 cup finely chopped green onion, white part only

1 cup frozen corn kernels, thawed and patted dry

1 **Coat an 8 1/2 x 4 1/2 x 2 1/2-inch loaf pan with cooking spray.** Set aside.

2 **In a medium bowl, combine flour, cornmeal, sugar, baking powder, salt, and cayenne.** Stir until well blended.

3 **In a small bowl, combine buttermilk, egg substitute, and the oil.** Whisk until completely blended. Add to flour mixture with the green onion. Stir until just moistened. Do not overmix. Place the batter in the loaf pan and sprinkle the corn evenly over all.

4 **Place a small wire rack, or 3–4 foil balls made from sheets of foil about 12 x 6 inches, in the bottom of a 6-quart slow cooker.** Put the loaf pan on top. Cover and cook on high only for 1 1/2 hours or until wooden pick inserted comes out clean.

5 **Turn off the heat and let stand 5 minutes, uncovered, before removing from the pan.**

Chunky Cherry-Peach Preserves

Makes 1 3/4 cups
Serves: 14
Serving Size: 2 tablespoons

**Exchanges/
Food Choices:**
1 Fruit

Calories	50
Calories from Fat	0
Total Fat	0g
Saturated Fat	0g
Trans Fat	0g
Monounsaturated Fat	0g
Cholesterol	0mg
Sodium	0mg
Potassium	27mg
Total Carbohydrate	13g
Dietary Fiber	1g
Sugars	10g
Protein	0g

Nonstick cooking spray

1 pound frozen unsweetened peach slices, thawed and chopped

3/4 cup dried cherries or dried cranberries

2 cinnamon sticks

1 tablespoon plus 1 teaspoon cornstarch

2 tablespoons water

2 tablespoons sugar

1 teaspoon vanilla extract

1/2 teaspoon almond extract

1 **Lightly coat a 3 1/2- to 4-quart slow cooker with cooking spray.** Stir in the peaches, cherries, and cinnamon sticks. Cover and cook on high for 2 hours, or on low for 4 hours, or until cherries are very tender.

2 **Remove and discard cinnamon sticks.** Combine the cornstarch and water in a small bowl and stir until cornstarch is completely dissolved. Stir into the peach mixture. Cover and cook on high for 15 minutes or until thickened slightly.

3 **Pour the peach mixture in a shallow pan, such as a pie pan, to cool completely.** When cooled, stir in the remaining ingredients. May serve immediately or refrigerate leftovers in an airtight container.

Cook's Note:
The mixture will continue to thicken as it cools.

Baked Pear-Apricot Fruit Spread

Makes 1 cup
Serves: 16
Serving Size: 1 tablespoon

**Exchanges/
Food Choices:**
1/2 Fruit

Calories	25
Calories from Fat	0
Total Fat	0g
Saturated Fat	0g
Trans Fat	0g
Monounsaturated Fat	0g
Cholesterol	0mg
Sodium	20mg
Potassium	57mg
Total Carbohydrate	5g
Dietary Fiber	1g
Sugars	3g
Protein	0g

Nonstick cooking spray

2 cups diced firm pears

1/3 cup diced dried apricot halves

1 teaspoon grated orange zest

1 tablespoon orange juice or water

1/2 teaspoon ground cinnamon

1/8 teaspoon ground cloves

2 tablespoons packed brown sugar substitute, such as Splenda

1 teaspoon vanilla extract

1/8 teaspoon salt

1 **Lightly spray a 2-cup glass heat-proof measuring cup with cooking spray.**

2 **Stir together the pears, apricots, orange zest, orange juice, cinnamon, and cloves into the measuring cup.** Place inside a 3 1/2- to 4-quart slow cooker. Cover and cook on high for 2 1/2 hours, or on low for 5 hours, or until apricots are tender.

3 **Carefully remove the measuring cup.** Stir in the remaining ingredients. Put the pear mixture in a shallow pan, such as a pie pan, and refrigerate at least 1 hour to cool completely.

Cook's Note:
You may store leftovers in an airtight container in the refrigerator for up to 1 month.

CHAPTER 12

Desserts

Cherry-Pear "Dump" Cake

Strawberry-Kiwi Cake in a Pot

Ooey Gooey Big Brownie Bowl

Pumpkin-Chocolate Chip Snack Bread

Individual Peach-Pineapple Crumblers

Apple-Peach Granola Crumble

Cobbler-Bottom Apple Bake

Triple Berry Dumpling-Style Shortcake

Rustic Peach Rice Pudding

Pumpkin Pie Pot Pudding

Individual Egg Custards with Fresh Mango

Cherry-Spiced Fruit Compote on Frozen Yogurt

Nutty Apple Halvers

Baked Ginger Pears with Sweet Cream Sauce

Cranberry Pomegranate Applesauce

Cherry-Berry Topping

Peanutty Chocolatey Dipping Sauce

Cherry-Pear "Dump" Cake

Makes about 4 cups
Serves: 9
Serving Size: about 1/2 cup

**Exchanges/
Food Choices:**
2 1/2 Carbohydrate
1 1/2 Fat

Calories	240
Calories from Fat	90
Total Fat	10g
Saturated Fat	1g
Trans Fat	0g
Monounsaturated Fat	5g
Cholesterol	0mg
Sodium	190mg
Potassium	159mg
Total Carbohydrate	38g
Dietary Fiber	3g
Sugars	23g
Protein	2g

Nonstick cooking spray

1 1/2 pounds diced firm pears or Granny Smith apples

14.5-ounce can tart pitted cherries

1 1/2 tablespoons sugar substitute, such as Splenda

1 tablespoon lemon juice

1/2 teaspoon almond extract

9-ounce box yellow cake mix

1/4 cup canola oil

1 **Coat a 6-quart slow cooker with cooking spray.** Place the pears, cherries, sugar substitute, lemon juice, and almond extract in the slow cooker.

2 **Stir to blend; sprinkle evenly with the dry cake mix.** Drizzle the oil evenly over all. Cover and cook on high for 3 hours.

3 **Turn off the heat, remove the lid, and let stand 1 hour to absorb flavors and some of the liquid.**

Strawberry-Kiwi Cake in a Pot *BACK COVER*

**Makes 2 cakes and
5 cups fruit**
Serves: 12
Serving Size: 1/6 cake,
2 tablespoons whipped
topping, about 1/3 cup fruit

**Exchanges/
Food Choices:**
2 Carbohydrate
1/2 Fat

CAKE
9-oz. box yellow cake mix

1/2 cup water

2 tablespoons canola oil

2 egg whites

1 tablespoon grated
orange or lemon zest,
optional

Nonstick cooking spray

Parchment paper or wax
paper

TOPPING
1/4 cup apricot or
raspberry fruit spread

1 1/2 cups sugar-free
whipped topping

4 cups whole
strawberries, quartered

2 ripe medium kiwi,
peeled and diced

4 teaspoons sugar
substitute, such as
Splenda, *optional*

1 **In a large bowl, combine the cake mix, water, oil, and egg whites.** Using an electric mixer, mix according to package directions. Stir in the zest.

2 **Coat a 3 1/2- to 4-quart slow cooker with cooking spray.** Cut a sheet of parchment paper or wax paper about 15 inches in length. Place the paper inside the slow cooker and press the paper to the bottom of the slow cooker and up the sides, pressing down folds. Note: this will not be even, but it will protect the cake from browning too much.

3 **Coat the paper with cooking spray.** Pour the batter into the slow cooker and smooth evenly. Cover and cook on high only 70 minutes or until wooden pick inserted comes out almost clean.

4 **Immediately remove the cake by lifting up on the edges of the paper and place on a wire rack for 15 minutes.** Gently peel the paper away from the cake and discard paper. Cool completely on wire rack.

5 **Using a serrated knife, cut the cake in half crosswise, creating two rounds.** Place each, cut side down, on a separate plate.

6 **Place the fruit spread in a small microwave-safe bowl and microwave for 20 seconds or until slightly melted.** Stir and spoon 2 tablespoons on top of each cake. Using the back of the spoon spread a thin layer evenly over the top of each cake.

7 **Spoon the whipped topping evenly over the top and sides of each cake and top with the strawberries and kiwi.** Sprinkle the sugar substitute evenly over all, if desired. Cut each cake into 6 wedges.

Calories	170	Sodium	150mg
Calories from Fat	45	Potassium	149mg
Total Fat	5g	Total Carbohydrate	29g
Saturated Fat	0.5g	Dietary Fiber	2g
Trans Fat	0g	Sugars	16g
Monounsaturated Fat	2.5g	Protein	2g
Cholesterol	0mg		

Ooey Gooey Big Brownie Bowl

Makes 6 cups
Serves: 12
Serving Size: 1/2 cup

**Exchanges/
Food Choices:**
1 1/2 Carbohydrate
1 Fat

Calories	160
Calories from Fat	50
Total Fat	6g
Saturated Fat	1.5g
Trans Fat	0g
Monounsaturated Fat	2g
Cholesterol	0mg
Sodium	150mg
Potassium	105mg
Total Carbohydrate	22g
Dietary Fiber	3g
Sugars	10g
Protein	3g

Nonstick cooking spray

1/2 cup all-purpose flour

1/2 cup white whole-wheat flour

2 teaspoons baking powder

3 tablespoons canola oil

1/3 cup semi-sweet chocolate chips

1/3 cup packed brown sugar substitute blend, such as Splenda

1/2 cup cocoa powder, divided

1 1/2 teaspoons vanilla, butter, and nut flavoring **or** 2 teaspoons vanilla extract

1/4 teaspoon salt

1/3 cup fat-free milk

2 egg whites

1/3 cup granulated sugar

1 cup strong hot coffee **or** 1 cup hot water plus 1 1/2 teaspoons instant coffee granules

1 cup fresh raspberries

1 **Coat a 3 1/2- to 4-quart slow cooker with cooking spray.** Mix together the flours and baking powder in a large bowl and set aside.

2 **Combine the oil and chocolate chips in a medium microwave-safe bowl and microwave on high for 30 seconds.** Stir with a fork until melted.

3 **To the chocolate mixture, add brown sugar, 3 tablespoons cocoa, vanilla, butter, and nut flavoring, salt, milk, and egg whites.** Add mixture to the flour and combine until well mixed. Pour the batter into the prepared slow cooker. Spread to smooth surface.

4 **In a medium bowl, whisk together the sugar, remaining cocoa, and hot coffee.** Mix until the sugar is dissolved. Pour the mixture over the batter in the slow cooker. Do not stir. Cover and cook on high only for 1 hour or until wooden pick inserted about 2 inches deep comes out clean.

5 **Remove the insert from the slow cooker and place on wire rack.** Sprinkle with berries and let stand 15 minutes before serving. Spoon into dessert bowls. Note: the bottom will be very runny, like chocolate syrup.

Cook's Note:

If not serving immediately, spoon onto a serving plate and spoon the syrupy mixture on top of the brownie mixture later. Refrigerate leftovers and reheat in microwave 30 seconds.

Pumpkin-Chocolate Chip Snack Bread

Makes 1 loaf
Serves: 16
Serving Size: 1/2-inch slice

**Exchanges/
Food Choices:**
1 1/2 Carbohydrate
2 Fat

Calories	200
Calories from Fat	80
Total Fat	9g
Saturated Fat	2g
Trans Fat	0g
Monounsaturated Fat	3g
Cholesterol	0mg
Sodium	125mg
Potassium	66mg
Total Carbohydrate	22g
Dietary Fiber	3g
Sugars	9g
Protein	4g

Nonstick cooking spray

1 3/4 cups white whole-wheat flour

1/3 cup packed dark brown sugar substitute blend, such as Splenda

1/3 cup granulated sugar

2 teaspoons baking powder

1/4 teaspoon baking soda

2 teaspoons pumpkin pie spice **or** 1 1/2 teaspoons ground cinnamon plus 1/2 teaspoon ground nutmeg

1/8 teaspoon salt

1 cup canned pumpkin

1/2 cup fat-free plain yogurt

4 egg whites

1/3 cup canola oil

2 teaspoons vanilla extract

1/2 cup chopped walnuts

1/2 cup mini semi-sweet chocolate chips

1. **Coat an 8 1/2 x 4 1/2 x 2 1/2-inch loaf pan with cooking spray.** Set aside.

2. **In a large bowl, stir together the flour, brown sugar, sugar, baking powder, baking soda, pumpkin pie spice, and salt.**

3. **In a medium bowl, whisk together the pumpkin, yogurt, egg whites, oil, and vanilla.** Stir in the walnuts and chocolate chips. Add the pumpkin mixture to the flour mixture. Stir until the flour mixture is just blended. Don't overmix; the batter should be slightly lumpy. Spoon into the loaf pan, gently smoothing the top.

4. **Place a small wire rack, or 3–4 foil balls made from sheets of foil about 12 x 6 inches, in the bottom of the slow cooker.** Put the loaf pan on top.

5. **Cover and cook on high only for 2 1/2 hours or until a wooden pick inserted in the center comes out clean.** Let cool for 5 minutes.

6. **Using a metal spatula, loosen the bread from the pan.** Turn out onto a cooling rack and let it cool completely.

Cook's Note:
This recipe can only be cooked on high setting. The slow cooker acts as an oven and the higher heat is needed to bake the bread properly. Flavors improve overnight. Refrigerate leftovers in airtight container for up to 1 week or freeze for up to 1 month.

Individual Peach-Pineapple Crumblers

Makes 4 ramekins
Serves: 4
Serving Size: 1

**Exchanges/
Food Choices:**
3 Carbohydrate
1 1/2 Fat

Calories	300
Calories from Fat	70
Total Fat	8g
Saturated Fat	0.5g
Trans Fat	0g
Monounsaturated Fat	4.5g
Cholesterol	0mg
Sodium	115mg
Potassium	230mg
Total Carbohydrate	43g
Dietary Fiber	5g
Sugars	22g
Protein	6g

FILLING
Nonstick cooking spray

2 cups unsweetened frozen peach slices

8-ounce can pineapple tidbits, packed in own juice, drained

1/4 cup fat-free sour cream

1/4 cup egg substitute

1 1/2 teaspoons lemon juice

1/2 teaspoon vanilla, butter, and nut flavoring or vanilla extract

1 1/2 teaspoons packed brown sugar substitute blend, such as Splenda

1/2 cup white whole-wheat flour

TOPPING
2 tablespoons sugar

2 tablespoons packed brown sugar substitute blend, such as Splenda

1/4 cup white whole-wheat flour

1/4 teaspoon ground cinnamon

1/8 teaspoon salt

2 tablespoons canola oil

1 Coat four 6-ounce ovenproof ramekins with cooking spray.

2 **In a medium bowl, combine all the filling ingredients, except the flour.** Toss gently until well blended. Add the flour and stir. Spoon equal amounts into each ramekin and set aside.

3 **In the same medium bowl, using a fork, stir together the topping ingredients, except the oil.** Drizzle the oil evenly over all and toss gently until crumb texture is reached. Spoon equal amounts over each ramekin.

4 **Place the ramekins in a 6-quart slow cooker.** Cover and cook on high only for 2 1/2 hours. Remove cover and continue to cook 30 minutes or until top is set.

5 **Serve warm or room temperature.**

Cook's Note:
These are great "portion control" desserts to help you indulge without the guilt!

Apple-Peach Granola Crumble

Makes 3 cups apple mixture and 1 cup whipped topping
Serves: 8
Serving Size: about 1/3 cup apple mixture plus 2 tablespoons whipped topping

Exchanges/ Food Choices:
1 1/2 Carbohydrate
1 Fat

Calories	180
Calories from Fat	50
Total Fat	6g
Saturated Fat	0.5g
Trans Fat	0g
Monounsaturated Fat	2.5g
Cholesterol	0mg
Sodium	90mg
Potassium	185mg
Total Carbohydrate	24g
Dietary Fiber	4g
Sugars	12g
Protein	3g

Nonstick cooking spray

1 pound tart apples, such as Granny Smith, sliced into 1/2-inch wedges

8 ounces frozen unsweetened peaches, thawed

1/4 cup packed brown sugar substitute blend, such as Splenda

1 teaspoon ground cinnamon

1/4 teaspoon ground nutmeg

1 teaspoon vanilla, butter, and nut flavoring **or** 1 1/2 teaspoons vanilla extract

1/8 teaspoon salt

2 tablespoons trans-fat-free margarine

1 1/4 cups low-fat granola, coarsely crushed

1/2 cup sliced almonds, toasted

1 cup light whipped topping

1 **Coat a 3 1/2- to 4-quart slow cooker with cooking spray.**

2 **In a large bowl, stir together the apples, peaches, brown sugar, cinnamon, nutmeg, vanilla, butter, and nut flavoring, and the salt.**

3 **Place the apple mixture in the slow cooker.** Cover and cook on high only for 2 hours or until apples are tender.

4 **Turn off the heat.** Remove cover; place small pieces of the margarine over the top. Sprinkle with the granola and almonds and let stand, uncovered, 30 minutes to absorb flavors and thicken slightly. Serve with whipped topping.

Cook's Note:

For a crunchier crumble, sprinkle the granola and the almonds on top *after* the apple mixture has cooked 2 hours. For a softer texture, sprinkle the granola and the almonds *before* the apple mixture has cooked and cook 2 hours.

Cobbler-Bottom Apple Bake

Makes 4 cups
Serves: 8
Serving Size: 1/2 cup

**Exchanges/
Food Choices:**
2 Carbohydrate
1 1/2 Fat

Calories	230
Calories from Fat	60
Total Fat	6g
Saturated Fat	0.5g
Trans Fat	0g
Monounsaturated Fat	3.5g
Cholesterol	0mg
Sodium	130mg
Potassium	160mg
Total Carbohydrate	32g
Dietary Fiber	4g
Sugars	15g
Protein	4g

BASE
Nonstick cooking spray

1/2 cup white whole-wheat flour

1/2 cup all-purpose flour

2 tablespoons granulated sugar

1 teaspoon baking powder

1/4 teaspoon ground cinnamon

2 egg whites

1/3 cup low-fat buttermilk

2 tablespoons canola oil

TOPPING
1/4 cup packed brown sugar substitute blend, such as Splenda

2 tablespoons white whole-wheat flour

1/8 teaspoon salt

3 medium tart apples (about 1 pound total), such as Granny Smith, peeled, cored, and cut into 1/2-inch slices

1/4 cup raisins

1/4 cup chopped pecans, toasted

1 tablespoon lemon juice

1 teaspoon vanilla extract

1 **Coat a 6-quart slow cooker with cooking spray.**

2 **In a large bowl, combine 1/2 cups of flours, sugar, baking powder, and cinnamon.**

3 **In a small bowl, whisk together the egg whites, buttermilk, and oil.** Stir into dry ingredients just until moistened. Batter will be thick.

4 **Spread batter evenly onto the bottom of the slow cooker.** Note: the batter will be a fairly thin layer.

5 **In the same large bowl used for combining the flour mixture, combine the brown sugar with the remaining 2 tablespoons flour and the salt.** Add the remaining ingredients and toss until well blended. Spoon over batter.

6 **Cover and cook on high only for 2 hours until a wooden pick inserted into the cobbler comes out clean.** Turn off the heat, remove cover, and let stand 15 minutes.

Triple Berry Dumpling-Style Shortcake

Makes 4 cups
Serves: 8
Serving Size: 1/2 cup

**Exchanges/
Food Choices:**
3 1/2 Carbohydrate

Calories	170
Calories from Fat	5
Total Fat	0.5g
Saturated Fat	0g
Trans Fat	0g
Monounsaturated Fat	0g
Cholesterol	0mg
Sodium	430mg
Potassium	108mg
Total Carbohydrate	38g
Dietary Fiber	4g
Sugars	13g
Protein	4g

FILLING
Nonstick cooking spray

1/2 14-ounce bag frozen unsweetened blackberries

2 cups frozen unsweetened strawberries

1 cup frozen unsweetened raspberries

1 teaspoon vanilla extract

3 tablespoons sugar substitute, such as Splenda

2 tablespoons reduced-fat biscuit and baking mix

1/2 teaspoon ground cinnamon

TOPPING
1 cup reduced-fat biscuit and baking mix

2 tablespoons plus 1 teaspoon sugar, divided

1/2 cup low-fat buttermilk

3/4 teaspoon ground cinnamon

1. **Coat a 3 1/2- to 4-quart slow cooker with cooking spray.** Place the berries and the remaining filling ingredients in the slow cooker. Toss gently yet thoroughly to blend. Cover and cook on high for 2 hours, or on low for 4 hours, or until bubbly.

2. **In a small bowl, combine the remaining 1 cup baking mix, 2 tablespoons sugar, and buttermilk.** Stir until just blended. Spoon the batter on top of the berry mixture in 8 mounds.

3. **In a small bowl, combine the remaining 1 teaspoon sugar and the cinnamon.** Sprinkle evenly over the batter. Cover and cook on high for 20 minutes or until wooden pick inserted into the dumplings comes out clean.

4. **To serve, spoon dumpling into dessert dish.** Spoon berry mixture over dumpling.

Cook's Note:
The cinnamon sugar is sprinkled on top not just for taste, but also because the dumplings will not brown in the slow cooker as they would if baked in the oven and this gives them more color.

Rustic Peach Rice Pudding

Makes about 4 1/2 cups
Serves: 9
Serving Size: 1/2 cup

**Exchanges/
Food Choices:**
1 1/2 Carbohydrate
1 Fat

Calories	150
Calories from Fat	30
Total Fat	3.5g
Saturated Fat	0g
Trans Fat	0g
Monounsaturated Fat	2g
Cholesterol	0mg
Sodium	85mg
Potassium	133mg
Total Carbohydrate	20g
Dietary Fiber	2g
Sugars	6g
Protein	3g

Nonstick cooking spray

2 cups water

1 cup uncooked brown rice

1/2 cup dried cherries

2 teaspoons ground cinnamon

1/4 teaspoon salt

3/4 cup fat-free half-and-half

2 teaspoons vanilla extract

1/4 cup packed brown sugar substitute blend, such as Splenda

8 ounces frozen unsweetened peaches, thawed and halved

2 teaspoons grated gingerroot

2 ounces sliced almonds, toasted and coarsely crumbled

1 **Coat a 3 1/2- to 4-quart slow cooker with cooking spray.**

2 **Place the water, rice, cherries, cinnamon, and salt in the slow cooker.** Stir until well blended. Cover and cook on high for 1 1/2 hours, or on low for 3 hours, or until rice is fluffy and liquid is absorbed.

3 **Stir in the remaining ingredients, except the almonds.** Sprinkle with the almonds. Let stand 5 minutes, uncovered, to absorb flavors. Serve warm for peak flavors.

DESSERTS DESSERTS DESSERTS DESSERTS DESSERTS DESSERTS DESSERTS DESSERTS DESSERTS DESSERTS DESSERTS DESSERTS DESSERTS DESSERTS

DESSERTS

Pumpkin Pie Pot Pudding

Makes 4 cups
Serves: 8
Serving Size: 1/2 cup
pudding plus 1 tablespoon
whipped topping

**Exchanges/
Food Choices:**
2 1/2 Carbohydrate
1 Fat

Calories	210
Calories from Fat	40
Total Fat	4.5g
Saturated Fat	0.5g
Trans Fat	0g
Monounsaturated Fat	2g
Cholesterol	0mg
Sodium	360mg
Potassium	142mg
Total Carbohydrate	39g
Dietary Fiber	3g
Sugars	24g
Protein	5g

Nonstick cooking spray

15-ounce can pumpkin

1 1/2 cups fat-free half-
and-half

2/3 cup packed brown
sugar substitute blend,
such as Splenda

1/2 cup reduced-fat
biscuit and baking mix

4 egg whites

2 tablespoons canola oil

2 teaspoons pumpkin or
apple pie spice

1/4 teaspoon salt

1 teaspoon vanilla, butter,
and nut flavoring

1/2 cup fat-free whipped
topping

1   **Coat a 3 1/2- to 4-quart slow
cooker with cooking spray.**

2   **In a large bowl, stir together all the
ingredients, except the whipped
topping, until well blended.**

3   **Pour into the slow cooker.** Cover
and cook on low only for 6 hours or
until knife inserted comes out clean.

4   **Turn off the heat.** Remove cover
and let stand 2 hours or until
completely cooled. Serve topped
with whipped topping.

Cook's Note:
This may be served immediately, if
desired. For a more "pie" taste and
texture, serve room temperature or
chilled. Refrigerate leftovers.

Individual Egg Custards with Fresh Mango

Makes 4 custards
Serves: 4
Serving Size: 1/2 cup
custard, 1/4 cup mango, and
2 tablespoons kiwi

**Exchanges/
Food Choices**:
2 1/2 Carbohydrate

Calories	180
Calories from Fat	5
Total Fat	0.5g
Saturated Fat	0g
Trans Fat	0g
Monounsaturated Fat	0g
Cholesterol	0mg
Sodium	115mg
Potassium	420mg
Total Carbohydrate	38g
Dietary Fiber	2g
Sugars	32g
Protein	5g

5 cups water

Nonstick cooking spray

1/2 cup egg substitute

1/3 cup pure maple syrup

2/3 cup fat-free milk

1/2 cup fat-free half-and-
half

1/2 teaspoon vanilla,
butter, and nut flavoring
or 1 teaspoon vanilla
extract

1/8 teaspoon ground
nutmeg

1 ripe medium mango,
peeled, seeded, and
diced

1 ripe medium kiwi,
peeled and diced

1 **Bring water just to a boil in a
medium saucepan.** Pour the water
into a 6-quart slow cooker. Coat
4 ovenproof ramekins or custard
cups with cooking spray and place
in slow cooker.

2 **In a 2-cup measuring cup, whisk
together the eggs, syrup, milk, half-
and-half, the vanilla, butter, and
nut flavoring, and the nutmeg.** Pour
equal amounts in each of the cups.
Cover and cook on low only for
3 1/2–4 hours or until knife inserted
comes out clean.

3 **Turn off the heat, remove the
cover, and let stand 15 minutes to
cool.** Remove the cups from the hot
water. Place on wire rack to cool.
When cooled, cover and refrigerate
until time of serving. Serve topped
with the diced mango and kiwi.

Cook's Note:
You can also serve this dish as flan
by running a knife around the outer
edges of the custards and inverting
them onto dessert plates. Surround
the flans with the fruit.

Cherry-Spiced Fruit Compote on Frozen Yogurt

Makes 2 2/3 cups fruit mixture
Serves: 8
Serving Size: 1/3 cup fruit mixture and about 1/3 cup frozen yogurt

Exchanges/ Food Choices:
2 Carbohydrate

Calories	160
Calories from Fat	15
Total Fat	1.5g
Saturated Fat	0g
Trans Fat	0g
Monounsaturated Fat	0.5g
Cholesterol	0mg
Sodium	125mg
Potassium	94mg
Total Carbohydrate	28g
Dietary Fiber	1g
Sugars	25g
Protein	5g

Nonstick cooking spray

1 cup chopped tart apple, such as Granny Smith

8-ounce can pineapple tidbits in own juice

8 ounces frozen peach slices, thawed and halved

1/4 cup dried tart cherries

1 teaspoon ground cinnamon

1/4 teaspoon ground allspice

1/8 teaspoon salt

1 1/2 tablespoons packed brown sugar substitute blend, such as Splenda

2 tablespoons trans-fat-free margarine

3 cups fat-free vanilla frozen yogurt

1   **Coat a 3 1/2- to 4-quart slow cooker with cooking spray.** Place apples, pineapple and its juices, peaches, cherries, cinnamon, allspice, and salt in the slow cooker. Gently stir until well blended.

2   **Cover and cook on high for 1 1/2 hours, or on low for 3 hours, or until apple is tender.**

3   **Gently stir in the brown sugar and margarine.** Serve over frozen yogurt.

Cook's Note:

For a thicker consistency, mix 1 tablespoon water with 2 teaspoons cornstarch and stir into the cooked mixture. Cover and cook on high for 10 minutes or until thickened slightly.

Nutty Apple Halvers

Makes 4 apple halves and about 1/2 cup topping
Serves: 4
Serving Size: 1 apple half plus 2 tablespoons topping

**Exchanges/
Food Choices:**
1 Carbohydrate
1 Fat

Calories	100
Calories from Fat	60
Total Fat	7g
Saturated Fat	1g
Trans Fat	0g
Monounsaturated Fat	3g
Cholesterol	0mg
Sodium	55mg
Potassium	56mg
Total Carbohydrate	11g
Dietary Fiber	1g
Sugars	7g
Protein	1g

Nonstick cooking spray

1 tablespoon trans-fat-free margarine

1/4 cup chopped pecans

1 tablespoon plus 1 teaspoon raisins

1/4 teaspoon apple pie spice or ground cinnamon

2 medium red apples, halved and cored

2 tablespoons sugar-free caramel ice cream topping

1 **Coat a 3 1/2- to 4-quart slow cooker with cooking spray.** Place the margarine, pecans, raisins, and pie spice in the slow cooker. Turn the slow cooker on low to melt margarine. When margarine begins to melt slightly, stir until well blended.

2 **Place the apple halves on top, overlapping slightly, if necessary.** Cover and cook on high for 1 hour and 15 minutes, or on low for 2 1/2 hours, or until apples are tender.

3 **Carefully remove the apples with a slotted spoon and place cut side up on a serving platter.** Stir the ice cream topping into the remaining ingredients in the slow cooker until well blended and spoon over all.

Baked Ginger Pears with Sweet Cream Sauce

Makes 4 pear halves and 1/2 cup sauce
Serves: 4
Serving Size: 1 pear half and about 2 tablespoons sauce

Exchanges/ Food Choices:
2 Fruit
1 1/2 Fat

Calories	180
Calories from Fat	60
Total Fat	7g
Saturated Fat	1g
Trans Fat	0g
Monounsaturated Fat	3.5g
Cholesterol	0mg
Sodium	45mg
Potassium	307mg
Total Carbohydrate	26g
Dietary Fiber	5g
Sugars	16g
Protein	1g

Nonstick cooking spray

2 tablespoons water

2 large firm pears (8 ounces each), cut in half lengthwise and core removed

1/4 cup chopped pecans, toasted

1/4 cup chopped dried apricots

4 teaspoons trans-fat-free margarine

2 teaspoons grated gingerroot

1/4 cup fat-free half-and-half

1 tablespoon packed brown sugar substitute blend, such as Splenda

1/2 teaspoon vanilla extract

1 **Coat a 3 1/2- to 4-quart slow cooker with cooking spray.** Pour the water into the slow cooker. Arrange the pear halves in the slow cooker, cut side up. Sprinkle equal amounts of the pecans and apricots over the pear halves.

2 **In a small bowl, stir together the margarine and the ginger.** Spoon equal amounts of the margarine mixture on top of each pear half. Cover and cook on low for 2 1/2 hours, or on high for 1 1/4 hours, or until just tender.

3 **Using a slotted spoon, carefully remove the pears and place in four individual dessert bowls.** Spoon the half-and-half evenly over all.

4 **Stir the brown sugar and vanilla into the pan drippings and spoon over all.**

Cook's Note:
Be careful not to overcook the pears or they will become mushy.

Cranberry Pomegranate Applesauce

Makes 3 cups
Serves: 9
Serving Size: 1/3 cup

**Exchanges/
Food Choices:**
2 Fruit

Calories	110
Calories from Fat	0
Total Fat	0g
Saturated Fat	0g
Trans Fat	0g
Monounsaturated Fat	0g
Cholesterol	0mg
Sodium	0mg
Potassium	196mg
Total Carbohydrate	29g
Dietary Fiber	4g
Sugars	22g
Protein	0g

3 pounds (8 cups total)
Granny Smith apples,
peeled, halved, cored,
and chopped

1/2 cup pomegranate
juice

1 whole cinnamon stick
or 3/4 teaspoon ground
cinnamon

1/4 teaspoon ground
allspice

1/2 cup dried cranberries

1 1/2 teaspoons sugar
substitute, such as
Splenda, *optional*

1 teaspoon vanilla

1   **Stir together the apples, juice,
cinnamon stick, and allspice in a
3 1/2- to 4-quart slow cooker.**
Cover and cook on high for
2 1/2 hours, or on low for 5 hours,
or until apples are very tender.

2   **Turn off the heat.** Stir in the
cranberries. Cover and let stand
30 minutes. Stir in the sugar
substitute and vanilla.

3   **Serve warm or chilled.** Cool
completely before storing in an
airtight container in refrigerator
for up to 2 weeks.

DESSERTS

Cherry-Berry Topping

Makes 3 cups
Serves: 9
Serving Size: 1/3 cup

**Exchanges/
Food Choices:**
1 Carbohydrate

Calories	80
Calories from Fat	0
Total Fat	0g
Saturated Fat	0g
Trans Fat	0g
Monounsaturated Fat	0g
Cholesterol	0mg
Sodium	0mg
Potassium	105mg
Total Carbohydrate	12g
Dietary Fiber	2g
Sugars	8g
Protein	1g

Nonstick cooking spray

12 ounces frozen unsweetened dark sweet cherries

1 pound frozen unsweetened mixed berries

1/4 cup pomegranate juice

1/4 cup packed brown sugar substitute blend, such as Splenda, divided

2 tablespoons water

1–1 1/2 tablespoons cornstarch

1/2 teaspoon grated orange zest

1/2 teaspoon vanilla extract

1 **Coat a 3 1/2- to 4-quart slow cooker with cooking spray.** Place the cherries, berries, juice, and 2 tablespoons brown sugar in the slow cooker. Stir gently. Cover and cook on high only for 2 1/2 hours or until cherries are tender.

2 **In a small bowl, stir together the water and cornstarch until the cornstarch is completely dissolved.** Gently fold into the fruit mixture with the zest, being careful not to break down the fruit, and cook 30 minutes or until thickened. Remove cover; stir in the remaining brown sugar and extract.

3 **Serve warm or chilled.** Store cooled leftovers in refrigerator in an airtight container for up to 2 weeks.

Cook's Note:
May serve over 1/2 cup fat-free plain Greek yogurt, 1/3 cup low-fat ice cream, or 1/2 cup diced cantaloupe or ripe pear slices per serving.

Peanutty Chocolatey Dipping Sauce

Makes 1 1/2 cups
Serves: 12
Serving Size: 2 tablespoons

**Exchanges/
Food Choices:**
1 1/2 Carbohydrate
1 1/2 Fat

Calories	120
Calories from Fat	60
Total Fat	7g
Saturated Fat	1.5g
Trans Fat	0g
Monounsaturated Fat	3.5g
Cholesterol	0mg
Sodium	110mg
Potassium	103mg
Total Carbohydrate	12g
Dietary Fiber	1g
Sugars	5g
Protein	4g

Nonstick cooking spray

2/3 cup regular peanut butter

1/4 cup sugar-free caramel ice cream topping

1/4 cup sugar-free chocolate ice cream topping

1/3 cup fat-free milk

1 teaspoon vanilla

1 **Coat a 2-cup glass measuring cup or ovenproof bowl with cooking spray.** Place all the ingredients in the measuring cup. Place the cup in a 3 1/2- to 4-quart slow cooker.

2 **Cover the slow cooker and cook on high for 1 1/2 hours, or on low for 3 hours, or until the peanut butter is melted.**

3 **Carefully remove the cup from the slow cooker, using a pot holder.** Place the sauce in a shallow serving bowl to cool slightly.

Cook's Note:
Store cooled leftovers in an airtight container for up to 2 weeks in refrigerator. To reheat, place in a small saucepan over medium heat about 2–3 minutes or until heated through. Do not bring to a boil. Or microwave in a heatproof container 20–30 seconds or until warm.

INDEX